JUGTOWN POTTERY

by JEAN CRAWFORD

JUGTOWN POTTERY

History

and

Design

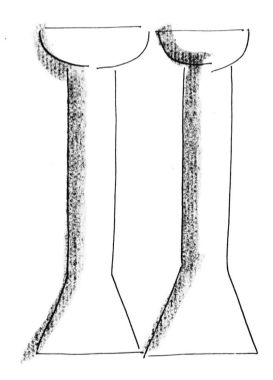

JOHN F. BLAIR, *Publisher* WINSTON-SALEM 1964

Library of Congress Catalog Card Number: 64-8376

ACKNOWLEDGMENTS

From the beginning, compiling the colorful story of Jugtown was a pleasant, absorbing experience. Not only was the subject itself of great interest, but the people with whom I worked were co-operative, helpful, and, above all, enthusiastic about the Jugtown story. To these of the many people who helped with this story I wish to express my sincere appreciation:

To Ben Owen for his time and patience in explaining and demonstrating the processes of pottery-making and in answering questions on Jugtown, and to his family for their generous hospitality;

To Boyce Yow, who explained the firing processes;

To Claud Scott for information on the early history of Jugtown;

To the long list of Jugtown supporters, museum personnel, writers, and arts and crafts personnel who were interviewed or responded to letters of inquiry and who supplied necessary information and gave moral support;

To the staff at the North Carolina Department of Archives and History and at the State Travel Bureau for having photographs made;

To Ben F. Williams, Curator, and William A. Martin, photographer, and to other persons at the North Carolina Museum of Art for their help in collecting information and taking photographs;

To Stephen G. Conrad of the North Carolina Department of Conservation and Development for making visual analyses of clay samples;

To the late John Maré for access to the Busbee files and for his personal interest and help;

To Woodrow W. Pruett for access to his personal letters from Juliana Busbee and for many interesting Jugtown tales;

To William Bridges for help in developing the personality of Juliana Busbee;

To Valerie Nicholson for suggestions on the manuscript;

To Clarence Thompson for the loan of pieces of his Jugtown Pottery for photographing and for his remembrances of the Busbees;

To Herbert F. Seawell, Jr., for access to his files on Jugtown;

To Howard C. Broughton for information involving the future of Jugtown;

To Russell Thompson for information on the Busbees and for color prints;

To Mamie H. Braddy for the use of a photograph;

To Lena P. Albright for suggestions on the design section of the manuscript;

To Noma Hardin for her suggestions on the manuscript, particularly on the design of Jugtown Pottery;

To Madeleine B. Street for her helpful suggestions on the manuscript;

To Blackwell P. Robinson for access to his files on the Busbees and Jugtown and for assistance on the manuscript, particularly on many historical questions;

To Bruce Roberts for his generous contribution of outstanding photographs;

To Clara Ridder for her invaluable guidance, sound suggestions, and continued encouragement and confidence;

And especially to John Fries Blair who made this book possible and with whom work has been a valuable experience, a challenge, a pleasure.

PHOTOGRAPH CREDITS

CONTENTS

List of Illustrations

Introduction

Part I━━━━━━━━━━━━━━━━━━━━━*History of Jugtown Pottery*

1 EARLY POTTERS IN THE JUGTOWN AREA   3

    Origin
    The Growth and Decline of Pottery-making

2 GROWTH OF JUGTOWN POTTERY, 1917-1947   10

    Early Efforts of the Busbees to Revive Pottery-making
       in North Carolina
    Search for Potters and Pottery in the Piedmont
       Section of North Carolina
    Introducing Pottery to the New York Market
    Jugtown Pottery Is Made and Sold
    Growth and Recognition Encouraged by Publicity
    Death of Jacques Busbee

3 JUGTOWN POTTERY SINCE 1947   37

    Movement by State Agencies to Save Jugtown
    Formation of Jugtown, Incorporated
    Formation of Jacques and Juliana Busbee's
       Jugtown, Incorporated
    Ben Owen Leaves Jugtown
    Lawsuit and the Closing of Jugtown
    Court Decision and the Reopening of Jugtown

4 RECOGNITION GIVEN JUGTOWN POTTERY   56

    Museum Collections
    Exhibits and Lectures
    Sales
    Written Recognition
    Appraisal by Authorities in the Art Field

Part II━━━━━━━━━━━━━━━Composition and Design of Jugtown Pottery

5 CLAYS   69
     Visual Analyses

6 FORMS   74
     Utilitarian Shapes
     Translations from the Chinese, Persian, Korean

7 SURFACE FINISHES   80
     Colors of the Glazes
     Enrichment

8 PROCESSES   85
     Preparing Clay
     Turning
     Glazing
     Firing

Part III━━━━━━━━━━━━━━━━━━━━━━━━━━━Prospect

9 THE FUTURE OF JUGTOWN   99

Notes

Bibliography

ILLUSTRATIONS

Color Plates ──────────────────── following page 80

I INTERIOR OF THE BUSBEE CABIN

II JUGTOWN POTTERY ON DISPLAY IN SALES CABIN

III JUGTOWN POTTERY IN ORANGE

IV JUGTOWN POTTERY IN "TOBACCO SPIT"

V JUGTOWN POTTERY IN YELLOW AND ORANGE

VI JUGTOWN POTTERY IN MIRROR BLACK

VII JUGTOWN POTTERY IN WHITE

VIII JUGTOWN POTTERY IN SALT GLAZE

IX JUGTOWN POTTERY IN "FROGSKIN"

X JUGTOWN POTTERY IN CHINESE BLUE

XI JUGTOWN POTTERY IN CHINESE BLUE

XII JUGTOWN POTTERY IN CHINESE BLUE

Black-and-White Illustrations ──────────────────

1 JACQUES BUSBEE 14

2 THE LIVING ROOM OF THE BUSBEE CABIN 22

3 POTTERY IN THE SALES CABIN AT JUGTOWN 25

4 JULIANA BUSBEE STANDING IN FRONT OF THE SALES CABIN 52

5 BOYCE YOW REMOVING CLAY FROM THE PUG MILL 71

6 SELECTIONS FROM THE JACQUES BUSBEE MEMORIAL COLLECTION ... 76

Top row (left to right) Pair of candlesticks—"Tobacco Spit," 12″ x 5″; covered soup tureen—orange, 7″ x 10″; jam jar with cover—salt glaze with cobalt blue decoration, 5 1/8″ x 6 1/2″; medicine jar with cover— "Frogskin," 6 1/8″ x 5″. Middle row (left to right) Bowl—"Frogskin," 3 1/4″ x 7 3/4″; vase—white, 11 1/8″ x 5 3/4″; Ming tree bowl—white, 4″ x 7″; bowl with fluted edge—white, 4 3/4″ x 11″. Bottom row (left to right) Jar with four handles and rope decoration—Chinese blue, 13 1/2″ x 9 3/4″; jar with two handles—Chinese blue, 12″ x 10″.

7 SELECTIONS FROM THE JACQUES BUSBEE MEMORIAL COLLECTION   77
*Top row (left to right) Flare vase—white with light cobalt blue lining,
7 1/4" x 8 3/4"; vase—white, 5 1/4" x 7"; "lily" vase with four handles—
white 9 3/4" x 7 1/2"; jar with four handles—salt glaze, 5 3/4" x 5 1/4".
Middle row (left to right) Grueby jar with four handles—"Frogskin,"
7" x 6"; tea bowl—"Frogskin," 2 1/2" x 5"; bowl—white, 3 7/8" x 12";
vase—salt glaze with white "drip," 7 1/4" x 4". Bottom row (left to right)
Chinese wine jar with incised decoration—salt glaze, 6" x 7 1/2"; vase
with two handles—white, 9 1/2" x 9"; Korean bowl—salt glaze with dog-
wood design in white, 3 1/16" x 8 13/16".*

8 KICK WHEEL AT JUGTOWN   86

9 THE KILN AND BEN OWEN COMING FROM THE CABIN WHERE HE
MADE POTTERY   88

10 BEN OWEN CHECKING POTTERY BEFORE PUTTING IT INTO THE KILN   90

11 BEN OWEN AND CHARLES MOORE STACKING BEAN POTS IN THE
GROUNDHOG KILN   92

12 A DENSE BLACK SMOKE RISES FROM THE GROUNDHOG KILN DURING FIRING   94

13 STILTS AND DISCARDED POTTERY IN FRONT OF THE GROUNDHOG KILN   102

INTRODUCTION

To many, the story of Jugtown Pottery is not new. It has been told by many writers and raconteurs in many versions. Each account—written and spoken—has increased the fame of Jugtown until today the story is almost a legend in North Carolina history. Yet up to this time there has been no thorough, comprehensive account of the place, the pottery, and the people identified with Jugtown. This book attempts to present the true, complete story. Every effort has been made to get information from authoritative sources and to sift the truth from years of wide, and often exaggerated, publicity.

The Busbees' personal collections of manuscripts, clippings, letters, and other records, dating back to the early 1900's, in the files of both Blackwell P. Robinson and the late John Maré were carefully examined. Juliana Busbee's letters to Woodrow W. Pruett were borrowed for reading. County records in the Moore County courthouse were scrutinized. Documents and legal papers on Jugtown from the files of Herbert F. Seawell, Jr., and P. H. Wilson were reviewed. Books, periodicals, newspapers, and files were studied in the libraries of the Woman's College of the University of North Carolina, the University of North Carolina (North Carolina Collection), the North Carolina Department of Archives and History, and the North Carolina Museum of Art.

Letters were written to museums and special groups throughout the United States and England to determine the extent of recognition given Jugtown Pottery through exhibits and collections. Arts and crafts groups and numerous individuals were written to establish points about the history and design of Jugtown Pottery.

Persons having knowledge of the history and pottery of Jugtown were interviewed. Some of the Busbees' closest and oldest friends provided valuable bits of unrecorded information on the Busbees and on life at Jugtown which helped to clarify and enrich many points in the story.

Many trips were made to Ben Owen's shop to observe him making pottery as he had at Jugtown. Many persons in the Jugtown area and persons who were directly or indirectly associated with Jugtown Pottery were consulted and probed for information.

Private and museum collections of Jugtown Pottery were studied. The collection of Jugtown Pottery in the North Carolina Museum of Art was studied with care.

Clay samples representative of those used at Jugtown were obtained. From these samples visual analyses of the clay were made at the Department of Conservation and Development, Raleigh, North Carolina.

All these data were checked, sifted, organized, and the result is this story of Jugtown and its pottery.

The story of Jugtown Pottery should be of interest to all North Carolinians, as it is a part of their cultural and historical heritage. It is the tale of two prominent Raleigh citizens who gave up their professions to go to the backwoods of Moore County to revive the dying pottery industry. It is the success story of a folkcraft which brought business to the state and fame, dignity, and refinement to North Carolina pottery.

This story may be of particular interest to historians, artists, and craftsmen who appreciate the pioneers in their fields—the brave in heart, the men and women who have a dream and who work to make that dream a reality.

The historian can see in the Jugtown tale the struggle to save a craft which had roots in the 1700's. Folkcraft pottery, made first to meet the domestic needs of the early settlers, was indigenous to the culture. Yet the habits of the people and the laws of the state changed, and the pottery industry suffered. The drama of the near-death and the revival of this colonial craft is interwoven in the tale of Jugtown.

The artist can enjoy the simple design of a hand-turned pot or vase and the vivid, distinctive colors which characterize this pottery. He can understand the application of art to life by a couple devoted to an ideal.

The craftsman can sympathize with the founders and potters of Jugtown in their contest to maintain a handicraft in the face of mechanization. He can admire the honesty and dignity of a potter dedicated to his work.

To those people who knew Jacques and Juliana Busbee personally, who felt the magnetism of their personalities, who dined with them in colonial comfort before their open hearth, this book will bring back many pleasant memories. Those who on a visit to Jugtown were fortunate enough to watch Ben Owen turn a Chinese vase or to see the door opened on a newly-fired kiln of ware need little orientation. This will be a visit with old friends, a promptbook for reminiscing on unforgotten days.

Those people who may not have heard of Jugtown but who themselves seek adventure in life or in the pages of history can live vicariously the Busbees' venture.

To the many who own Jugtown Pottery, this story can enhance their pride of ownership. These collectors will strengthen their knowledge of the pottery and look upon their pieces with new interest.

The student of ceramics may find the section on design of especial value. He can study this pottery and the traditional methods by which it was made for inspiration in his own work.

In the last analysis, all of us must judge the significance of the pottery by its design. Examples of both the design and the elements affecting the design—the clays, the forms, the surface finishes, the processes used in making the pottery—are included for the study and enjoyment of Jugtown Pottery.

PART I
History of
Jugtown
Pottery

ONE

Early Potters in the Jugtown Area

Origin

The time was late in the nineteenth century; along the old plank road from Fayetteville to Bethania,[1] potters' shops hummed with busy "kick wheels." In the rural community of upper Moore County, North Carolina, pottery-making was a lucrative business, with potters at work turning crocks, "dirt dishes," churns, whiskey jugs, and other domestic wares. James H. Owen, a potter from Moore County who died in 1923, remembered thirty-five potters who were his contemporaries at the end of the nineteenth century.[2]

Unfortunately, the name and the date of arrival of the first potter in this section are clouded in obscurity. Conflicting reports have been given, but documentary evidence is insufficient to support any one theory exclusively.

In 1926, Ivan Stowe Clark, in writing the history of the little corner region of "southeastern Randolph, southwestern Chatham, northwestern Moore, and northeastern Montgomery counties . . . an area of approximately 20 square miles . . . a population of about 150 people," said:

It was in the early part of the 18th century that a group of plain people, potters by trade, landed in the vicinity of Jamestown, Virginia, and gradually moved inland into the "Piedmont Section" of North Carolina. Some of these pioneers drifted into this region now called "Jugtown" about 1750.[3]

A. F. Greaves-Walker, an authority on ceramics, wrote more specifically on the early North Carolina potters:

The first pottery in North Carolina of which we have record was that started by Peter Craven in the Steeds section of Moore County in 1750. Craven was an English potter from Staffordshire and located on a small farm where he both tilled his land and made utensils for himself and his neighbors, using surface clays from the surrounding country.

A few years later a Moravian potter, name unknown, located near Hickory and made pots, jars and utensils in his spare time.

We have no further records until 1861 when we find Doris Craven, the fourth in the Craven line, still operating a little farm pottery near Steeds. It is interesting to note that the descendents [sic] of the first Craven are still making pottery in the same section.[4]

This same author wrote that in 1750 settlers from

near Staffordshire, England, landed at the port of Wilmington, and went through the pine forests of the coastal plains to the western edge of the royal grants, which had preempted all the land for 150 miles from the coast.[5]

Mrs. Jacques Busbee, who helped her husband found Jugtown Pottery, contradicted this authority's claim that the potters landed on the North Carolina coast. She wrote that her husband, Jacques, had concluded from his study of

old books, tombstones, land deeds, and from signed statements of old, old men dead these past 12 years . . . that the potters of hereabouts came south from Virginia, possibly for safety from the Indians. According to reliable authority, pottery was made in Virginia prior to 1649. . . . We have used the date 1750 because we had a pitcher signed and dated bearing that date. There is where the 1750 date sprang into being.[6]

Another writer advances the idea that the potters may have come through the colony of Pennsylvania. This writer proposed that there were a

half dozen of the original Staffordshire Englishmen who came, either directly into the province, or through the colony in Pennsylvania, which sent thirty thousand emigrants to North Carolina about the middle of the century when they became disgruntled with the Penns over the tax laws imposed upon them.[7]

The earliest contemporary reference to pottery made in North Carolina, except that made by the Indians, is found in the records of the Moravian congregations at Bethabara and Salem, the earlier of which dates back to 1752. Church records, personal diaries, memorabilia, and other records of these Moravian settlements were translated from German into English by a recent archivist. In the church diary, references begin in November, 1755, to mention pottery-making. A potter's shop was built in February, 1756, and by August of that year Gottfried Aust, the potter, fired the first earthenware in his kiln.[8]

In connection with a search for graffito and slip ware, two investigators traced German pottery-makers from Pennsylvania to a Weaver family in a community near Hickory, North Carolina, known as Jugtown.[9] A group of Hickory citizens supported the idea that the first pottery designated as Jugtown was made in Catawba County, beginning with Jack Weaver, a German.[10]

In 1947 one writer traced the history of the first potters in the area of Moore and Randolph Counties through Rafe (Raffe) Cole and Pater Craven.[11] He claims that Rafe Cole, a potter from Lancashire, England, came to America before or after Revolutionary times and settled in the northwestern area of Moore County. Rafe taught his son, Evin Cole, the potter's trade, and Evin located not far away in Randolph County, near Seagrove. Pater Craven, from Pennsylvania, settled near Steeds before the Civil War and taught the potter's trade to his son, J. D. Craven.[12]

R. E. Wicker, who has done historical research on the Piedmont section of North Carolina, wrote that the Cravens were from Randolph County.

There were no Cravens in either Moore or Cumberland until comparatively recent times.

From my own recollection, which runs back some sixty years, the potters in the jugtown [sic] area were the Owens, Teagues, and somewhat later, the Coles.

.   .   .   .

Judging by their names, it would appear to me that the Cravens were Dutch, the Owens, Welsh, and the Coles, perhaps English.[13]

But probably the most extensive research on early North Carolina potters was done by Jacques Busbee. He found the potters in North Carolina to fall into three groups:

The Catawba County "Dutch," the remnants of the Forsyth County Wilkesboro Moravians: the potters around Asheville who were not native potters (with one exception) and the potters descended from the Staffordshire settlers in the section where Moore, Randolph, and Montgomery Counties join.[14]

His records contain letters in shaky script and in stilted English from men who knew the local potters. He transcribed his notes into an account book, the most authentic record found to date on the potters in the Steeds area. Mr. Busbee referred to the information compiled in this record book, which he referred to as his "notebook," [15] in articles for the press and in his own writings.

Mr. Busbee traced the earliest potter in the Steeds area to Peter Craven, from Staffordshire, England, who came to North Carolina from Pennsylvania before the Revolution. Peter Craven, the patriarch of the line of potters in this area, was the father of J. A. Craven, who had three children: Enoch S., a potter; a daughter who married a Fox; and J. Anderson, a potter, born around 1802.[16]

Mr. Busbee's records make no reference to Enoch's having had children. J. A. Craven's daughter, who married a Fox, had two sons, James and Tom, who were potters. James Fox was the first potter to escape military service in the Civil War by working at his pottery shop, where he made bowls, mugs, medicine jars, and telegraph insulators for the Confederacy. Major [John] Sloan [17] of Greensboro provided him with an assistant. James and his younger brother Tom were considered the best potters in the section—the southern edge of Randolph County.[18]

J. Anderson Craven had four sons who were potters: J. Dorris, W. Nicholas, Thomas,[19] and John A. J. Dorris and Nicholas turned pottery for Hardy Brown, who had a kiln in the northwest corner of Moore County on the old plank road. During the War they made cups and saucers and dishes for the Confederacy. Their stoneware was decorated with blue smalt.[20]

According to Jacques Busbee, J. Dorris Craven had three sons who carried on the family tradition: Daniel Z., I. Frank, and J. Anderson.[21] However, men in the area today say that only Daniel made pottery. Franklin had a shop but hired others to make the ware for him, and J. Anderson was not a potter.[22]

Another potter, Chester Webster, started a shop in Randolph County prior to 1853. He came to North Carolina "from the North," which locally meant "anywhere from out of the county." [23] One letter described his ware as "distinctly Flemish—my pitcher is ornamented with childish drawings of birds and flowers, with scalloped bands and handle decorated at its juncture with the pitcher." [24]

Pottery-making thus appears to have been a family craft which was handed down from father to son, generation after generation. The Craven family, following the family trade begun by Peter Craven, were still making some ware in 1917 when Jacques Busbee began his research to locate potters. Other families in the area were also turning pottery at the end of the nineteenth century. Among the names which Mr. Busbee lists were Chrisco, Cole, Cagle, Davis, Garner, Handcock, King, Moody, McNeill, Moffitt, Meekins, Owen, Richardson, Spencer, Scott, Spinx, Suggs, Teague, Tucker, Yow.[25]

The Growth and Decline of Pottery-making————————————

The pottery shops of a hundred years ago were unlike the potteries in the same area today. They were not commercial stores with display or sales rooms but merely places to turn pottery. The potters usually turned ware only when they found time from their farm work. The products were articles for domestic use, such as crocks, churns, pickle jars, teapots. Some of this ware was unglazed, and some was finished with a salt glaze on the gray stoneware or a transparent glaze on the orange earthenware.

The wares were loaded on covered wagons and sold by "waggoners" to general stores, to warehouses, or from door to door. Moving slowly through North Carolina, South Carolina, and Virginia, the waggoners were gone two or three weeks, and sometimes months, at a time. The pottery was either sold for a few cents—for example, jugs sold for from five cents to fifteen cents a gallon—or traded for needed merchandise, such as nails and horseshoes. Peanuts, onions, dried apples, tanned leather, and other foodstuffs were also taken along to sell.[26]

In death as well as in life the potter was served by his jugs. Jugs with closed tops and open bases served as grave headstones. While the clay was still malleable, an inscription was made on the jug. Many of these jugs have been removed, broken, or replaced by commercial markers, but a few remain today. In the Union Grove Churchyard, between Sea-grove and Robbins, eight jug headstones remain, dated 1838, 1895, 1896, 1897, 1898, 1918, 1932, and 1938.[27] One clay marker in the "Jugtown burying ground" was supposed to have been dated 1750.[28] On one jug tombstone a potter paid his wife a humble, yet fitting, tribute: "She done the best she know'd how."[29]

As the whiskey industry grew in North Carolina, the output of "little brown jugs" increased, and the pottery industry grew large and profitable. At the last of the nineteenth century between fifty and sixty[30] individual pottery shops were turning out jugs, as well as some domestic wares. The sale of jugs far exceeded that of household wares, for women had begun to buy white "chiney"[31] and glass fruit jars.

In 1908 [32] the adoption of prohibition dealt a crippling blow to the pottery industry of North Carolina. Pottery shops were silent as men were forced to turn to farming and to working in sawmills and factories.[33] The craft which had lasted 150 years, "uninfluenced by the outside world," [34] seemed doomed.

TWO

Growth of Jugtown Pottery 1917—1947

Early Efforts of the Busbees to Revive Pottery-making in North Carolina

"Jugtown" was a word of derision fifty years ago. Any community making jugs was a jugtown; this was not an "honorific title," [1] especially during prohibition. A person would not have found Jugtown on the map, and had he asked the direction to Jugtown he would have been sent on a rainbow search. [2]

The story of Jugtown Pottery began with such a search—a search by Jacques Busbee which was to develop into a lifetime venture.

Jacques Busbee (n. James Littlejohn Busbee [3]) was born in Raleigh, North Carolina, on May 20, 1870, the son of Charles Manly and Lydia Littlejohn Busbee. The Busbee family was prominent in Raleigh, and the name Busbee was especially outstanding in the field of law. In 1914, when the Busbee home was being torn down, a newspaper article said:

Much of the history of Raleigh, and sidelights of history, have centered about this house. Here many of the distinguished men and women of the past century have been entertained. Courtly speech, charming grace, and the lingering splendour of the Old South held sway in this castle until they were memories. Henry Clay was entertained here upon a visit to the city. Here he was feted, and in those walls the pride of old Raleigh lingered upon the words of the matchless orator and the statesman. And there were others, celebrities of the South and of the North who came and were greeted with the hospitality of the place.[4]

Jacques Busbee's interests, however, were not in the field of law but in the field of art. A North Carolina historian wrote of his artistic temperament: "A near genius, and like other men touched lightly with the divine spark, he has quaint and queer traits, characteristics and mannerisms."[5] He studied at the National Academy of Design, the Art Students' League, and the Chase School, all in New York, and was by profession a portrait painter. He was sent to Roanoke Island by the North Carolina Historical Commission in 1907 to paint scenes along the coast for the Jamestown Exposition.[6] In addition to being a painter, he was a lecturer[7] and a writer, centering his topics around North Carolina and art.[8]

In 1910 Jacques married Juliana (n. Julia Adeline Royster), the daughter of William Burt and Julia Tutt Royster of Raleigh.[9] Juliana, also from an old, distinguished Raleigh family,[10] attended St. Mary's Junior College for two sessions, studied photography under her uncle, and was an illustrator.[11]

In 1915, Mrs. Busbee, as Chairman of the Art Department of the Federation of Women's Clubs of North Carolina,[12] was promoting the folk-crafts of basketry, weaving, and pottery-making, rather than the fine arts in North Carolina. Mr. Busbee, while lecturing to schools, colleges, and clubs throughout the state, was making a study and collection of old pottery.

A search by the Busbees for old potters—the seed from which Jugtown grew—is a story that has been told in many versions. Whether it was Jacques or Juliana who began the search remains a point in question. According to Jacques Busbee, the articles of Mildred Harrington, who wrote for magazines and newspapers, were a "notable exception" to the varying reports by New York magazines and newspapers and the inaccurate coverage by state papers of the Jugtown story.[13] Miss Harrington tells the story that when Mr. Busbee was appointed to judge the art exhibits at the State Fair he wrote to every potter whose name he could get, asking him to send pottery. Most of the ware he received was "bad stuff," but there was enough good to know the "spark" was still there.[14]

Another account has been given more frequently. In 1915 Mrs. Busbee was a judge at a Davidson County Fair in Lexington. While helping to arrange a display of apples or while judging the display (two versions) she saw a "brilliant orange glaze pie plate." She rushed to the hardware store where the pie plate had been purchased and bought all the plates on the shelves—at ten cents each. Only a few plates were being made at that time, since most of the old potters had left their wheels for more lucrative jobs. Packing the pottery in her suitcase and shipping her clothes in a box, Juliana rushed to Raleigh to show Jacques her "discoveries." Not waiting to get home, she "unpacked the suitcase on the floor of the railroad station" to show him the dishes. His enthusiasm for the orange pie dishes matched her own.[15]

Juliana wrote later of their "pie plate" journey:

It was that empty pie plate we set sail in, on an adventurous journey. And it has taken us for a long ride, bumpy sometimes, but always interesting. We were like the owl and the pussy cat who went to sea in a beautiful pie plate, instead of a pea green boat, and it landed on shores just as amazing.[16]

The crusade to save the dying industry began. The Busbees lectured to their friends and sought out potters and educators, but few people in the state showed any interest. With fruitless returns for their efforts, the Busbees decided to present their ideas to another market—New York.

We plunged headlong into a strange and seemingly crazy performance, with no money—no encouragement—and against the advice of every single human being who knew us. We had as a stimulant what we term passionate patriotism.[17]

Soon afterwards, about 1916, the Busbees moved to New York, intending to spend a year. With the nation involved in World War I, portrait work was scarce, so Jacques wrote short stories and articles.

He believed that art should be a democratic expression, & that if we as North Carolinians were to develop a native art, the handicraft must be reckoned with—and that fine art should be the flowering of a folk art. And—when no one else would revive the pottery craft—& it was a craft— not an art—he would be very grand & do the work in a year or so & present it to the State & then return to portraits. . . . Then he came to realize that it was a better contribution to our state to help the country potters & show them a new way for old jugs than to paint portraits of dead & gone heros & dignitaries from photographs.[18]

Encouraged by the "artists and ceramic experts" in New York who saw their pottery collection, the Busbees, "without funds or backing," decided to try to put this "unique product of our state on the world market."[19]

First they needed a source and supply of pottery to sell for funds. They decided on the Moore County area "as the most interesting place"[20] to begin a search for old potters still making the ware.

Search for Potters and Pottery in the Piedmont Section of North Carolina

Some writers say the search for the maker of the orange pie plate began at Whynot, a village of thirty or forty citizens near Seagrove, but a letter from Mr. Busbee to the mayor of Whynot, inquiring about the potters there, failed to bring a reply. Mr. Busbee decided, if they were to locate the potters, they must go down to the area and find them. (Whynot, they discovered later, was unincorporated and had no mayor.)[21]

On May 1, 1917,[22] Jacques Busbee arrived at Seagrove, the station closest to the extreme northwest corner of Moore County—the "dark corner,"[23] as the people of southern Moore call the upper end

The natives, who seldom traveled out of the county, thought he was a Yankee. With the country plunged into World War I, some insisted he was a German spy. Mr. Busbee wrote of his arrival:

fig. 1 JACQUES BUSBEE

My trunk was checked from New York. That was sufficient evidence. The crowd of seven people who gathered to see me alight at the end of the whilom log road (but now carrying passengers as well), looked at me long and suspiciously. The station agent grunted ostentatiously as he lifted my trunk, heavy with books. Afterwards I heard that he held a consultation with the crowd as to the expedience of breaking open this piece of luggage which of course was filled with bombs to destroy the corn fields and to wreck the little cross road store. I was a German spy—that was self evident. One man in the crowd had seen a German once and he declared that I looked just like him! [24]

Juliana wrote that another thought he was "one of them Swedes. . . . That we are born and bred North Carolinians they have never believed and never will." [25] One native remembers that people were "scary" of the Busbees when they first came. [26]

Jacques Busbee gave an account of the community he found:

We found the country potters languishing, even [in] Moore [County], they were moribund—and stale. Prohibition laws of years standing were the cause. There was no longer any money to be made in the production of jugs. Where fifty kilns once made a good living with orders from the distilleries, a half dozen potters could now supply the country neighborhood with jugs for vinegar or sorghum syrup, with churns, crocks and butter jars, pitchers and stew pots. "Toy stuff" as the potters called table ware—the "dirt dishes" of the Civil War period—were not in demand, since white "chiney" was abundant and cheap. The price of ware had fallen to ten cents and lower, a gallon.

But "toy stuff" and "dirt dishes" of the Civil War period were . . . the only types of pottery that would have a present day use or a wide appeal.

The potters who were still operating their shops in this Saffordshire [sic] section were all men past middle life. They farmed on the side for a support, as there was little profit in ware making, even though the family did much of the work around the shop, and without pay. Even the wood for the kiln was cut on the potters' own land—as a rule—and cost only the labor.

The potters' sons, with generations of craftsmanship in their hands, were straying off to sawmills or to cotton and furniture factories, in fact, to any job that offered a living wage.

Between the time of our first visits some eight or ten years before, and our return in 1917 there was woeful falling off in the quality as well as the output. The potter had lost faith in himself as well as in his market. He had lost his tradition and was feebly attempting to imitate factory made stuff of the ten cent store variety in the desparate [sic] hope of getting back his market.[27]

The potters whom Mr. Busbee found still at work were few. Rufus Owen, son of Franklin Owen, a potter, was turning some stoneware and farming. He is said to have made the orange pie dish that aroused the Busbees' interest to begin their search.[28] In 1918, his brother, Jim Owen, a "Holy Roller" preacher and potter, was selling his ware for four cents a gallon—a ten-gallon jug or churn bringing only forty cents.[29] Paschal Morable, another old potter, was still at work.[30]

After locating the few remaining potters, putting the pottery on the market remained a problem for the Busbees. These older men were temperamental and unaccustomed to a rigid schedule. They filled orders so "spasmodically" that supplying regular orders to a New York outlet became difficult for the Busbees.[31]

To get the potters to make the simple ware that their fathers had made, rather than imitations of cheap dime-store ware, authentic examples of old pottery were needed as guides. An intensive search was begun by the Busbees for old ware to determine the "best local traditions." Wrote Jacques of his search:

My adventures with old Josh Sheffield (pronounced Shuffle) and his blind mare and buggy over a radius of 25 miles of where Jugtown Pottery is now established is a story in itself. We slept on corded bedsteads in log cabins, we ate the simple food that was offered with lordly hospitality, we rummaged in lofts and smokehouses and cellars for ware, and what could not be bought was sketched or photographed.[32]

Juliana has mentioned Old Josh Sheffield—or "Old Joe Shuffle" as he was called—in several of her articles. Supposedly, he was one of the old potters remaining in the township of Sheffield, in Moore County. He claimed Staffordshire descent, and to the Busbees' surprise was found to be named Josiah Wedgewood Sheffield. An old ballad has been handed down:

> Old man Shuffle he kicked a kick wheel
> Old man Shuffle turned pots on a wheel
> Old man Shuffle he kicked out a jug
> And drank from it all it would hold.

Juliana added, "The moral of the ballad is that he had delirium tremens and killed his pet drake thinking it was a snake." [33]

A local Moore County authority wrote:

The Sheffields were also probably English, but I do not recall any of that name being potters, though it is now claimed that they were, and that one was named Josiah Wedgewood Sheffield. I do not believe this claim can be supported.[34]

One native of the Steeds section remembered no Sheffields living in this section at the time Mr. Busbee came down.[35]

Most of the Busbees' search was over rough back roads, in an age before cars and paved roads in that section. About the part she played in obtaining documentary data on the pottery, Juliana wrote:

I will always count it the high spot of adventure in my careering when my husband and I in an old wagon—he in overalls driving the mule— and I with my camera set out by day break, day after day, to picture all that could be found. They would be all day trips with crackers and cheese . . . at midday.[36]

Their search through the neighborhood yielded ware that dated to "within two generations of Peter Craven." [37] They traced the genealogy of the potters through sales of household property, family Bibles, old books, land grants, and talks with the citizens of this section—men who remembered when potters "under guard" [38] made ware for the Confederacy.

Several of the old pieces of the pottery, signed, dated, and collected by Jacques Busbee, were reportedly from the eighteenth century, and some were from the nineteenth century.[39] The original pottery collected by the Busbees on these trips is reported to have been seen by visitors to Jugtown, but no one knows what happened to it. One person has suggested that Mrs. Busbee probably gave it away.[40]

After locating the few potters still turning ware and collecting original pieces of old pottery to compare with pieces then being made, the Busbees realized that the pottery industry was at a critical stage. If the potters' sons did not follow the family craft, pottery-making would be lost in the next generation. The Busbees presented this problem to groups and individuals in the state, but they were unable to arouse any interest or support. The choice had to be made by the Busbees as to whether or not to follow through with their "adventure." Jacques later wrote of his decision:

To train the younger men in a sense of beauty, form, fitness; to keep alive the most interesting folkcraft-tradition in the United States today, seemed to us a task undertaken for our state and worthy of any sacrifice involved.[41]

The sacrifice involved giving up their careers and selling their library, "reportedly the third most valuable collection of North Caroliniana." [42]

Introducing Pottery to the New York Market

They realized their best market would be New York, so Juliana and a Mrs. Bane opened a tearoom at 60 Washington Square, in the section known as Greenwich Village.[43] The Village Store, located in the basement of an old house,[44] cost forty dollars a month rent.[45]

The story is told that at the end of World War I General Pershing and his soldiers paraded through New York City, ending their march in the Village, where Juliana served tea to them from the Village Store.[46]

Several young girls from the South visited New York in the summer of

1918, and Juliana asked them to help her in the tearoom while Mrs. Bane was on vacation. One member of that group wrote:

Our help to Mrs. Busbee consisted of talking to the guests while they were having lunch. We found them very interesting and they enjoyed the little Southern girls and their Southern accent. Colored maids served the lunch. It was all very informal. It was there I learned to like paprika. . . .[47]

The only advertising was by word of mouth, but by 1919 the Village Store was attracting the attention of New Yorkers. Mrs. Busbee wrote:

I knew that food was not the sole element for a popular tea room. My servants did that. I believed if I could properly magnetize the shop, get the right people together, give the something to the place that one gives a home—that people would come—& believe me—they did.[48]

The ultimate goal of all who frequented the Village Store was the large round table at which Juliana Busbee presided. It became a rendezvous for young writers, among them Eugene O'Neill.[49] A guest at the round table might find himself seated next to anyone "from Rachmaninoff to Jackie Coogan, from fashionable preachers to Florida real estate speculators." [50]

The Busbees' plan was to use the Village Store to introduce pottery and other North Carolina crafts to the New York public. Jacques' responsibility was to have the products made by the potters and craftsmen and then shipped North. This meant that he spent many months each year in North Carolina, while Juliana lived most of the year in New York.

The first pottery orders to meet the New York demand were given to the older men who had their own kick wheels and kilns: Henry Chrisco, Rufus Owen, James Owen, and J. W. Teague.[51] These potters made the shapes that were familiar to them, the utilitarian pieces that had served their needs for many generations.

Other handmade articles from North Carolina were also sent to New York for sale. Near Steeds, but over the line in Moore County, in a community that had been almost self-sufficient, handmade furniture, baskets, cloth, and clothes were commonplace. Few families could afford the luxuries of manufactured items from the general store or from the mail order catalogue.

Martha Jane Scott, the mother of Claud Scott, a farmer from Steeds, had sheared, carded, spun, and woven wool into cloth for her family. Now she sent the handwoven cloth to Mrs. Busbee for sale at the Village Store. Another member of the Scott family, Bygie, a half-brother of Claud, had made furniture which was now shipped to the Village Store. Claud Scott did not know "how many hundred" split-bottom chairs Bygie Scott had made and sent North for sale.[52]

One newspaper article mentions some of the items sold at the Village Store in New York:

Practically everything in the Village Store is a Moore County product and much of the food served there is from "down home." The pottery, split-bottom chairs, the rugged tavern tables, the handwoven jeans, the shuck door mats, the hearth brooms, the gingham table covers . . . .[53]

While Juliana was getting established in New York, Jacques was adjusting to life in a community far from any cities. In these early years Jacques was living with families in the neighborhood. He stayed the first summer with Steve Richardson in Brower Township, Randolph County.[54] Then for several years he stayed with Henry Scott, a farmer, in Moore County. Each day Mr. Busbee walked back and forth from Mr. Scott's cabin to James Owen's pottery shop about a mile away to watch the ware being turned.[55]

From spring until around Christmas each year Mr. Busbee stayed with the Scotts; then he went to New York to spend the winter months. After the cabin at Jugtown was built, he stayed the entire year in North Carolina, going to New York only on short trips.[56]

Jugtown Pottery Is Made and Sold

In order to have greater control over the design and production of the pottery, Mr. Busbee decided about 1921 to set up a shop and hire potters to work for him. Up to this time no potter's shop, kiln, or building had been erected under the name of Jugtown.

In 1921 or 1922, Henry Scott and his son, Claud Scott, built the first structure of Jugtown—the shop. They followed the directions of the old potters, and the long cabin resembled the other shops in the community. The pottery shop at Jugtown met the few, simple needs of the potter: dirt floor, two kick wheels, board shelves for drying the ware, and a cast-iron stove.[57]

The shop was built on land owned by W. H. Scott and Martha Jane Scott and was leased to Jacques Busbee by an agreement signed on June 15, 1922. Mr. Busbee was to have the privilege of renting this shop for ten successive years, "commencing September 1922, at the rental of $50.00 a year." [58] A clause provided the right to use the "land adjoining the shop for the purpose of building additional or necessary buildings in the operating of this business." [59]

For two years Mr. Busbee leased the land; then he decided to buy it. On August 25, 1924, Mr. Scott and his wife, Martha Jane, sold seven and three-fourths acres to Jacques Busbee for $500.[60] Six acres were acquired from T. Franklin Scott and his wife, Eula E. Scott, on January 26, 1938.[61]

About two years after the shop was built, a log cabin was built by the Scotts for the Busbees. They used trees from a field close by.[62]

The log house, which was charmingly furnished with very old, handmade furniture [63] the Busbees had collected from the surrounding countryside, became an attraction to visitors. The cabin had wide-board wooden floors, walls of roughhewn logs and plaster, and low ceilings. The rustic, colonial atmosphere was played up by Mrs. Busbee by her rejection of modern conveniences and her emphasis on using handmade textiles, baskets, and pottery and wild flowers and greenery. Large open fireplaces were used for heat and, in the early years of Jugtown, for cooking. Corner cupboards and sideboards in the kitchen–dining room displayed the Busbees' collection of pottery; books lined the walls in the living room, and signed prints, drawings, and engravings hung on the walls. Bright orange curtains [64] were at the windows, and orange was repeated in the chair covers and the pottery.[65]

The house reflected the Busbees' interests and was an appropriate set-

fig. 2   THE LIVING ROOM OF THE BUSBEE CABIN

ting for the craft movement which they were promoting. A favorite theme
of Juliana was the relation of art to life. She wrote:

> *What greater compliment could be bestowed than to say of a person,
> He or she "has a genius for life"—that the surroundings and the individual
> are in harmony.*[66]

A reporter from New York recognized the finesse of the Busbees in
blending their refined tastes into an unobtrusive country setting:

. . . we pulled up before a charming log cabin built on simple lines so like—and yet so utterly unlike—anything seen in the entire countryside. Floating through the intense summer heat were the strains of Chaliapin's Volga Boat Song and on the long porch across the front of the Jugtown cabin were bright orange flower pots filled with velvety purple petunias, and in a tall floor jar by the door was a branch of pine—the whole thing so native and yet so strangely Japonesque—that it took my breath. . . .

Through the screen door I was amazed to see four men in overalls— smoking—two sitting at a card table playing checkers—the portable Sonora pouring out the strains of the world's greatest basso. One of the men was reading the New York Times—a baby in a large wicker hamper basket—the room beautiful in its fitness and use of native split-bottom chairs—a big open fireplace filled with wild flowers, while on the long tavern table was a soft gray jar filled with a bunch of native salmon colored orchids of entrancing beauty, unrivalled by anything in a Fifth Avenue florist's window—the room scattered with American and English magazines and papers.

Jaques Busbee [sic]—in overalls—came forward and met a hot, dirty, hungry traveller and I instantly recognized him as a man of the world. He introduced me to his wife, who was dressed in a pale yellow gingham which harmonized perfectly with the room—so perfectly that I knew the dress was no accident.[67]

The old potters, Mr. Busbee found, were "hard baked" and were unwilling or unable to accept new ideas or instruction on pottery design. Ben Owen, the son of Rufus Owen and a descendant of the Staffordshire potters,[68] remembered his father's comment about turning small pieces of pottery for the New York clientele: "I didn't want to fool with them little toys." [69]

When the operations began at Jugtown, the younger men of the community, rather than the older potters, were hired. "Young potters are more plastic and can assimilate art training that is the absolute essential for any craft with more than a parochial interest," wrote Jacques Busbee.[70]

Charlie Teague, a young man who had returned home from the first World War, the son of J. W. Teague, was the first potter at Jugtown.

He turned ware there for eight years, then moved on to work for other potteries.[71]

Ben Owen came to Jugtown in 1923, several months after operations had begun. He was only eighteen years old, but pottery-making was not new to him. As a child he had played around his father's shop and had stacked pottery in the kiln. He was a "ball boy" for his father, picking the clay clean and shaping it into balls, ready for turning. When his father was not at the kick wheel Ben would practice turning "small things." Ben's two brothers, Joe and Charlie, were potters, too, and in later years set up their own shop.[72]

Charlie Teague, his wife, and Ben Owen lived with Mr. Busbee in his cabin until about 1926, when Mrs. Busbee came down to Jugtown to live permanently. Ben continued to live with the Busbees until 1936, when he got his own log cabin and a wife, Lucille Harris.[73]

Young men in the neighborhood were hired to mix clay, cut and haul wood, fire the kilns, and help with other outdoor jobs. During the 1930's and 1940's Rancie Moore worked about fifteen years and Ernest Williams worked about twelve years as "outside workers" at Jugtown.[74]

The exact year when the stamp "Jugtown Pottery" was first used on the bottom of each piece of ware is not known. Ben Owen thinks the trade name was used shortly after operations began around 1922 or 1923.[75] Jacques Busbee wrote that the trade name "Jugtown Ware" was registered as a trademark;[76] however, investigation has failed to reveal that a trademark was applied for or issued until 1959, when Jugtown, Incorporated, had the name registered.[77]

When the present Jugtown first began operations, its output was almost exclusively the traditional, utilitarian shapes: plates, platters, pitchers, bowls, candlesticks, tea sets, pickle jars, milk crocks, bean pots, stew pots, butter jars, preserve jugs.[78]

Some years later Tiffany Studios in New York, a customer of Jugtown Pottery, suggested that they make some decorative pieces.[79] As an admirer of Chinese pottery, Jacques Busbee turned to the East for inspiration. He made frequent trips to museums and libraries in New York to study the ceramic arts of China and other countries famous for pottery.

fig. 3 POTTERY IN THE SALES CABIN AT JUGTOWN

Ben Owen once went with Mr. Busbee through these museums, examining and feeling the pottery while Mr. Busbee made sketches and notes.[80] The sketches and notes made during these trips could not be found for study; however, the Busbee library contains numerous books on pottery, especially Chinese pottery.

The Han, T'ang, and Sung dynasties Mr. Busbee considered to be the supreme eras in Chinese ceramics, and it was the pottery of these periods from which he gained his inspiration.[81]

In the Jugtown shop Ben experimented with the unfamiliar shapes, while Mr. Busbee stood by him, suggesting fullness here, an elongation there. Over and over again Ben turned a vase, only to have it fail the critical test. Although the work was difficult and slow, the two men worked together in harmony and had respect for each other's particular talents. The trained eye of the artist and the skilled hands of the potter together produced ware unfamiliar to North Carolina kick wheels. Gradually the number of Chinese, Persian, and Korean translations in the Jugtown selection increased, and in 1922 *House Beautiful*, in a feature article on Jugtown Pottery, said:

A titled Chinese gentleman begged a cracker jar to take home to add to his collection of ceramics because it bore a striking resemblance to early pieces made in central China.[82]

Growth and Recognition Encouraged by Publicity

The pottery was popular in the Village Store and elsewhere, and orders increased. As business grew, the Village Store moved uptown in New York—to 37 East Sixtieth Street.[83] An art magazine in April, 1923, carried this notice: "The little Village Store has recently moved away to larger and more attractive quarters, and Jugtown Pottery is looking up." [84]

The new Village Store was noticeably different from its surroundings. Juliana followed her "dramatic impulse" to put simplicity among the sophisticated.

. . . in the midst of fashionable N.Y., a simple country store—serving plain

N.C. food—on N.C. tables—with table cloths of N.C. gingham and on N.C. pottery plates & dishes.[85]

The Village Store became a gathering place for people in the art and literary fields. Among those who gathered around Juliana's round table in her uptown store were the Rockefellers, Mrs. Henry Ford, and Eleanor Roosevelt.[86] Juliana later wrote:

I used in the shop only native materials and therefore gathered artists, magazine editors, newspaper people, feature writers . . . whose friendliness and sympathy and interest made our little efforts bloom like the Bay tree. For they wrote about us—I mean the pottery—and every article written about Jugtown helped every potter in the state and advertised North Carolina.[87]

Articles appeared in magazines and newspapers about the Village Store, about the North Carolina folkcrafts, and especially about Jugtown Pottery. In 1923 the *New York Telegram* wrote:

But do you know Jugtown Pottery? If you do not you are the loser. . . . In this particular shop, the only one of its kind in New York, the most delightful pieces of pottery for every table and decorative need may be bought at the most astonishingly low prices.[88]

A woman of wit and intelligence, Juliana Busbee was featured by the New York papers as a remarkable business leader. She belonged to the Zonta Club of New York, a professional women's club which had such outstanding members as Lucille La Verne, Fannie Hurst, and Mrs. Charles Hawthorne.[89] She also belonged to the Fifth Avenue Association, composed of people having businesses along the famous avenue.[90]

The popularity of the pottery was spread by the press and by visitors to the Village Store, and orders increased. One letter from the Chief Clerk of the Shipping Department at the Village Store pleaded:

. . . will be glad to welcome 10 barrels a day for it seems the shelves are empty. Juliana hardly gets a shelf all out before some party or other spoils it by buying it bare.[91]

By the middle '20's Jugtown Pottery had received sufficient publicity in the New York area for one leading magazine to write:

There are probably still a few readers of THE NEW YORKER *who do not know about the Jugtown pottery, which is on sale in the tearoom of Mrs. Busby, at 37 East Sixtieth Street.*[92]

Columbia University, New York, had used Jugtown as the subject for a lesson in a book of reading tests for the fifth, sixth, and seventh grades.[93] Visitors from out of the state began stopping by Jugtown.

After the revival of the fading industry at Jugtown, other potters in the area returned to their kick wheels. Shops that had stood idle for years were opened; kilns that had grown cold were fired; new shops were built.

The neighborhood potters, curious to see the unfamiliar shapes being turned by Ben Owen, went over to Jugtown. They received no formal training from Mr. Busbee,[94] but they did leave with an interest in and an awareness of a variety of new shapes and glazes. The shapes these potters in the neighborhood now began turning were not entirely the utilitarian pieces their fathers had made. They developed new shapes and glazes which they thought would have commercial appeal.

Jacques in North Carolina, as well as Juliana in New York, was taking every opportunity to publicize the Jugtown story. On May 9, 1925, Jugtown gave a party—a party that is still remembered as a "big day" in Jugtown history. More than one hundred people were there—plain and fancy, countrypeople and city dwellers, world travelers and men who had never traveled more than a day's journey from home. A reporter captured the moment with this account:

Among those present were editorial writers from New York magazines; a delegation of Catawba Dutch potters, who had come to study the work of their fellow craftsmen; visitors from Pinehurst, Greensboro, other North Carolina cities, and the villagers themselves.

As a result there were flivvers parked next to covered wagons, overalls side by side with knickerbockers and "store pants." There were top knots demurely cloaked—picturesque sunbonnets, and there was bobbed hair. There was cigarette smoking, but there was more dipping of snuff.[95]

Following an old custom, each local man and boy wore a rose pinned to the bill of his cap—"their way of dressing up."

From 6 one morning until 6 the next there was jollification and feasting. There were fiddlers to play while they sang, with old-time energy, old songs like "I'm Agoin' Down the Road Afeelin' Bad" and "Keep My Skillet Good and Greasy."

Reportedly, they consumed 200 pounds of pig (barbecue), 35 chickens, and 2 bushels of cornbread.[96]

The Busbees' efforts to make Jugtown known were justified in sales as well as in publicity. Juliana's purpose in opening the Village Store had been to "introduce" Jugtown Pottery and to get a continuing market for the pottery. The shop had succeeded in its purpose. Juliana wrote:

From the first moment I opened that shop I never failed to pay expenses. . . . Jugtown has operated on its earnings from the beginning. We have never been a kept industry.[97]

The shop had set Jugtown on its feet. In 1926 Juliana sold the Village Store and moved back to North Carolina. She wrote, ". . . after 10 years our shop in New York was sold and I came down here in the backwoods 'for keeps' and to live happily ever after." [98]

With the reputation of Jugtown Pottery spreading, the number of visitors increased. Among visitors at Jugtown were the Baroness von Trapp,[99] the late John P. Marquand, and the late Dorothy Thompson.[100] Claud Scott said they came from all sections of the country. You could tell "by numbers on the cars." [101] Many people vacationing in the Pinehurst–Southern Pines area were attracted by the unconventional setting. During the late '20's and the '30's, officers from Fort Bragg frequently came down to Jugtown.[102] Professional and amateur ceramists and college and high school students in the ceramic arts made trips to Jugtown. Students from North Carolina State College were frequent visitors to watch Ben Owen at the kick wheel or to try their own skill at the potter's bench.[103]

One person said it was not unusual to see visitors from Russia, Japan, France, or some other foreign country at Jugtown. Juliana always pressed a piece of Jugtown Pottery into the hands of these special visitors for them to take back to their homes.[104]

Visitors were welcomed to Jugtown, and Juliana often invited them in to see the cabin, to have tea, and, if she was especially attracted to them, to stay for supper. However, if they were curiosity-seekers and Juliana felt that they did not share her love and appreciation for handmade pottery, she did not encourage them to stay. When interrupted from a pleasant visit with friends in her cabin, she was known to say with great firmness, "We're closed on the Sabbath!" Knowing full well that the day was Friday, the dumbfounded visitor could not protest.[105]

Dinner guests were frequent. One report said the Busbees averaged twenty guests a week for "food prepared by herself [Juliana], strictly in native fashion, on the open hearth." [106] Mrs. Busbee boasted of preparing the meals all on the open hearth but is said to have had a stove in her kitchen pantry.[107] Guests sometimes helped prepare the meal—by peeling potatoes, turning roasting apples, making coffee—so that a Jugtown dinner became "a very social occasion, not only in the eating but in the making." [108]

Also, after dinner Juliana would enlist the services of her guests. She would bring out two large bowls—one with warm, soapy water for washing dishes, one with clear water for rinsing. Then each guest was given a dishcloth to dry the dishes as Juliana washed them right at the table.[109]

One satisfied dinner guest wrote:

When you call on the Busbees you drink long forgotten rum toddies from quaint jugs, and your dinner is likely to be a pheasant boiled in the great fireplace, with crackling bread cooked in the ashes.[110]

Mrs. Busbee's recipes were in character with the rustic log cabin and the remote country setting. When she was entertaining a guest for the first time, she usually prepared food that was peculiar to the area, using recipes that had been popular fifty or seventy years before.[111] The recipes included candied yams, spoon bread, Brunswick stew à la Jugtown (using rabbit or squirrel), corn pone, 'simmon pudding, rice bread.[112] Possum was also served on occasion.[113] One frequent guest at Jugtown remembered that a "pot of beans" was always cooking on the hearth.[114]

Although many guests remember only Juliana's "country" dinners, she was also skilled at international cuisine and often served curried dishes and other exotic foods. She told the story that when she was young her family was not wealthy but her mother insisted that her children develop cultivated tastes and habits. Once a week she would serve a French dinner and the family would converse in French, or she would serve a Greek dinner and the conversation would center around Greece, or she would pick some other foreign country as the theme for the weekly dinner.[115]

Juliana knew food, books, music, flowers "like few people."[116] But probably her greatest love was books, for she said that if necessary she would move all her tables and beds out to make room for them. Books lined the walls of the living room in the log cabin: books on philosophy, religion, poetry, pottery, history, books autographed by their authors, rare editions. Juliana got up early in the morning so that she could read before visitors came, and she read late in the night. She loved poetry, and she and her friends would quote passages to each other by the hour. She told one friend that her favorite book was a copy of *Evangeline*, which she had kept in her pocket when she was a little girl and which she had read "through tears."[117] One close friend knew that she was especially fond of Emily Dickinson, and when, on occasion, he quoted her poems, Juliana "clapped her little hands and her eyes laughed with glee."[118]

She wrote of her great love of books:

Just think of what we take from every book we read. After we have digested what we have read, it is ours. . . . I am so sorry for those who do not love—and know—books.

.   .   .   .

I think the love of books is a very strong bond, even more than flowers and gardening. There is nothing competitive about literature—there is in gardening. Book lovers do not show off—they want to share.[119]

In later years when Juliana was alone she wrote that she was getting "knee deep" in a new book,

So I'm not lonely. However, I never am. It has always seemed to me that

lonely people were stupid ones. I do not see how a book lover can ever be lonely.[120]

While the kitchen was Juliana's stage, Mr. Busbee's talents were often evident out of doors. The Jugtown setting, always picturesque, was more interesting and colorful because of Mr. Busbee's green thumb. He had an iris garden of choice varieties in a full range of colors which people came out in the spring just to see. He also propagated hemerocallis, producing a pink variety.[121]

Juliana became well known for her flower arrangements. With a simple pine branch she could make an Oriental dish garden of great beauty. Using wild flowers from the fields and forests, or flowers from Mr. Busbee's garden, or pine boughs, or autumn leaves, she made arrangements that are remembered as "magnificent."[122] She became excited when she saw wild flowers growing along the road, especially when they were yellow or orange, her favorite colors. She said, "They're God's favorite colors, too, or why would He have made so many of them!"[123]

Mushrooms were also a hobby and an interest of the Busbees. Mrs. Busbee, who liked to use them in cooking, could distinguish the poisonous mushrooms from the edible varieties that grew around Jugtown. She told the tale that when she was a young girl she read an article on raising mushrooms and decided to grow some. Her sister Edith, who was more dignified than her younger sister, came into Juliana's bedroom one day and complained of a most unpleasant odor. Juliana assured her that it was nothing to worry about. "I'm only growing mushrooms," she said, and pulled out her dresser drawers to show her sister the mushrooms that she was cultivating in beds of manure.[124]

Animals were very much a part of the Jugtown scene. The Busbees always had dogs, usually named for characters in opera. Two German police dogs were named Loge and Erda, and the giant Schnauzer was called Hans (Sachs). Mr. Busbee also raised Chinese silkies, pheasants, and peacocks which strolled over the yards.[125]

The unconventionality of the Busbees was well known. Mr. Busbee was the first person in the area to wear Bermuda shorts. As early as the

1920's he wore tennis shorts made of oxford cloth in the summer, prompting laughter from neighbors and visitors.[126]

External appearances—clothes, make-up, hairdos—were of little concern to Juliana. She refused to wear "sto'-bought" clothes, but wore clothes that were handmade from lovely, hand-woven fabrics. Mary Hambidge and Cornelia Norwood made many of her costumes. Completing her "homespun" look, she always wore cotton stockings and low-heeled shoes. A friend remembered seeing her only once in silk stockings and high-heeled shoes, and then he had to laugh because she looked so unnatural.[127]

Once, on the way to a meeting at the North Carolina Museum of Art, she demanded that her escort stop the car and let her out to pick wild flowers along the roadside. With great unconcern, she walked into the meeting with her shoes covered with mud.[128]

When the Museum of Art had its grand opening, Juliana was asked to pour punch at the reception at the Governor's mansion. Having dressed hurriedly at the Sir Walter Hotel, Juliana emerged with her two-piece dress on wrong side outwards. Her escorts called attention to the error, but Juliana was indifferent. She saw no reason to change. Finally she was persuaded to reverse the blouse, but she wore the skirt to the reception with the wrong side out.[129]

In the dead of winter the water pipes at the Jugtown cabin sometimes froze and burst. Juliana, with her typical scorn of modern conveniences, did not become perturbed. Instead, she welcomed the inconvenience, saying, "Now I won't have to take a bath!" [130]

Many people were drawn to Jugtown by the stimulating conversations of the Busbees and by their entertaining stories. Mrs. Ernest L. Ives, who first met the Busbees about 1939, wrote:

I, of course, never drove anyone to call [on the Busbees] who wasn't fascinated. The stories were unique. . . . they were both eccentric and so full of imagination that many times the stories were hard to believe.[131]

Friends who had known them for many years would testify that Mrs. Busbee lived in an "ethereal" world.[132]

One of Juliana's favorite stories was about a woman who came to Jugtown and tried to impress Juliana by her pretentious manner. The woman was heavily corseted and wore thin stockings, and she immediately aroused Juliana's dislike. Seeing a flower on Juliana's hearth, the woman asked if it had an aroma. Juliana replied, "If the flower has a fragrance and you are an aristocrat you can smell the aroma, but if you are not an artistocrat there is no aroma." Quickly the woman got down on both knees to smell the flower, and as she did she burst both knees in her stockings and two staves in her corset. Triumphantly, the woman announced, "It has a most *glorious* aroma!" Juliana said later that the flower had no aroma at all.[133]

Juliana's dynamic personality attracted many people to her. Friends felt it a privilege when permitted to be her escort or when seated by her at a dinner. Whenever she appeared at public functions, at meetings of the Art Society, or at lectures or teas, crowds gathered around her. Getting her disentangled from groups of which she was the center was like getting a celebrity away from her fans.[134]

Juliana loved the parties and the attention of friends as well as the quiet of her cabin. In later years, when she was alone, she wrote:

I have been quite gay these past two or three weeks—lots of company here—have spent two nights in Southern Pines—three dinner parties— the kind that make me feel like Cinderella when she returns from the ball! However, I like the ashes.[135]

Jugtown grew to have special meaning for many people. It was more than a place where earthen wares were made and sold. A long-time friend of the Busbees summed up what many people felt: "Jugtown is hospitality as well as pottery." [136]

During the 1920's pottery shops had sprung up "like mushrooms," [137] and pottery-making was again a thriving industry in North Carolina. The "dark corner" of Moore County once more became recognized as a pottery center.

The Busbees have been credited by many writers with awakening the sleeping pottery industry. An instructor at a North Carolina university observed that "about 5 years ago [1921] . . . there was an increased demand for the wares. This was due partly to the efforts of Mr. Busbee and his wife . . . to make the art nationally known." [138]

He also wrote:

Thru the efforts of these two patrons of art [the Busbees] a national recognition for the inherent beauty of form and coloring of this pottery has been secured and a market found for it.[139]

A newspaper in 1927, in an article subtitled "Mr. and Mrs. Busbee Take First Step Toward Rehabilitating An Art and An Industry Almost Lost in Decay," said:

The thing has prospered. It was the first thing of its sort undertaken in the United States, and already the product is sold in every state in the Union, and some of it has been exported.[140]

Another writer considers the popularity of Jugtown under the direction of the Busbees to have been in part harmful to the North Carolina pottery industry.

Other potters, seeing that Jugtown ware sold well, set up roadside stands and proceeded to sell garishly-colored pots to the passing tourists, just as fast as they could possibly turn them out.[141]

During the depression of the '30's the potters kept working and not one was on Federal relief.[142]

The popularity of Jugtown Pottery continued to grow. Newspapers and state magazines featured Jugtown more frequently during the '30's and '40's. Carloads of clubwomen and busloads of children made pilgrimages to this remote community. Also, Mr. and Mrs. Busbee gave lectures on Jugtown Pottery to clubs, schools, and organizations, sometimes assisted by Ben Owen, who gave demonstrations on the potter's kick wheel.

North Carolina beamed with pride at the growth of her pottery industry, and the Busbees were praised for their labors and foresight in developing Jugtown Pottery. By setting high standards of quality for their pottery, and by encouraging publicity, they had helped other potteries as well as Jugtown. *The Christian Science Monitor* wrote:

*The Busbees showed the native potters that not only the charm, but the
pecuniary value, of their product lay in its indigenous character and the
individuality of workmanship.*[143]

Death of Jacques Busbee

On May 21, 1947, after a two-week illness, Jacques Busbee died of a
heart attack, ending a thirty-seven-year marriage which had been predicted
to fail. Juliana wrote:

*My family, the Busbee family, all our friends and relatives forecast
tragedy for the two J's. We had to make a success of our marriage—and
did, to their dismay. You see we had no money, & yet entertained more,
and had the gayest kind of time.*[144]

Jacques Busbee's death also ended a thirty-year venture in the pottery
industry. His influence had probably been in the art forms rather than
in the executions, as Juliana had written of him: ". . . his self-appointed
job was to give art training to the potter, to try to teach the potter to see
beauty of form and line and color." [145]

In December, 1947, Jacques Busbee was honored by a Memorial Exhibit of Jugtown Pottery at Person Hall at the University of North Carolina. The brochure for that exhibit describes Mr. Busbee as a man with
many interests, but, above all, as having an interest in the folk art of North
Carolina:

*Jacques Busbee was by profession a painter; but by choice he was a
hobbyist—landscape gardening, taxidermy, orchids, mushrooms, first editions, book binding, chickens, music, the Greek Drama, and Caroliniana
are a partial catalogue of his hobbies.*

.   .   .   .

*He believed that art is not an esoteric utterance but a democratic expres-
sion, that North Carolina should develop a native art, and that from folk
art, truly understood and expressed, fine art springs.*[146]

THREE

Jugtown Pottery Since 1947

Movement by State Agencies to Save Jugtown

In 1949 North Carolina took action to recognize Jacques Busbee by making a permanent collection of Jugtown Pottery for the State. Governor W. Kerr Scott wrote Mrs. Busbee on November 4, 1949:

> In behalf of the people of North Carolina, I wish to express an interest in the very significant collection of pottery left by your late distinguished and gifted husband.
>
> He made a unique contribution to our artistic and cultural development in this country and in this state in particular. The State of North Carolina would consider it a signal honor to give permanent recognition to this splendid collection of an ancient art that was revived in our own day and time. While no funds are available for the purpose at the present time, I am writing to suggest that an effort be made to work out an arrangement whereby Jugtown can be permanently preserved as a shrine for future generations.[1]

Later in November of the same year, the North Carolina State Art Society awarded posthumously a certificate in recognition of Jacques Busbee's contribution to art in North Carolina. At the presentation, Mrs. Katherine Pendleton Arrington, first President of the State Art Society, said: "Jacques Busbee did more for the development of art in hand-made pottery than anybody in North Carolina." [2]

In further recognition of Jacques Busbee, the State Art Society decided to assemble a permanent collection of Jugtown Pottery "somewhere in his native state." A committee was appointed with authorization from the Society to assemble the collection and present it to the State Art Society at its annual meeting in 1950. The committee was composed of Isabelle Bowen Henderson, Chairman; Robert B. Wynne; Lucy Cherry Crisp, Treasurer; Alexander Crane; and Ben F. Williams. [3]

The collection was made by individual contributions from the Busbees' friends. Pieces of pottery were received from private collections and cash donations were used to purchase pottery from Jugtown. [4] The collection, over one hundred pieces, [5] was exhibited at the State Art Gallery from December 1, 1950, through January 30, 1951. [6] Pieces of Jugtown Pottery were borrowed from the private collection of Clarence Thompson for exhibition at the same time. [7] The collection, known as The Jacques Busbee Memorial Collection of Jugtown Pottery, became a part of the permanent collection of the State Art Society and is preserved in the North Carolina Museum of Art.

Mrs. M. W. Crocker, a cousin of Juliana Busbee, has also given her collection of Jugtown Pottery to the North Carolina Museum of Art. [8]

From the beginning of Jugtown, Jacques had managed the business, handled orders, mixed and applied many of the glazes, and controlled the quality and design of the pottery. After Jacques' death, Juliana and Ben continued the operation at Jugtown. Juliana handled the finances and the correspondence. Ben had the primary responsibility for the pottery-making, although Juliana occasionally helped with the glazing. Boyce Yow ground and mixed the clay and stacked and fired the kilns. The orders continued to come in and business remained good.

Jugtown was never run as an organized business for making a profit. Juliana said that they kept no records of how many pieces of ware they produced in a day.

It is not how much is turned in a day's work, but how beautifully. . . . We do not know how many pieces are fired in the kiln, what proportion of loss nor how much profit. If we knew, we would have quit long ago.[9]

A newspaperman commented, "A North Carolina native pottery is probably the only place on earth now where willful inefficiency pays." [10]

Gradually, managing the business became burdensome and difficult for Juliana. More responsibility was assumed by Ben; he had to pay for necessary supplies and check the orders. It became obvious to many of Juliana's close friends that her memory was failing and that she was experiencing periods of confusion.[11]

Ben Owen looked for ways to help Juliana and to keep Jugtown operating. He made frequent efforts to communicate with Zebulon Judd in Auburn, Alabama, the husband of Juliana's sister, her only close relative. A month passed with no word from Dr. Judd. Mrs. Judd was critically ill and Dr. Judd could be of no real help.[12]

Realizing the need for outside help, Juliana took the initiative in seeking ways to continue operations at Jugtown. In letters and conversations she made appeals to her friends and to state agencies. In response, a movement to help Juliana and to save Jugtown was launched.

In 1958 Governor Luther B. Hodges asked Christopher Crittenden, Director of the Department of Archives and History, to study the possibilities of preserving Jugtown for the State in some manner.[13] Dr. Crittenden visited Mrs. Busbee in April and mentioned the State's interest. Mrs. Busbee was receptive to the idea, for she and Mr. Busbee had always hoped to contribute in some way to their native state.

Dr. Crittenden consulted with members of his staff and with other state agencies about the possibility of taking over Jugtown. Several suggestions for continuing the operation were considered. Mrs. Joye Jordan of the Hall of History felt that certain parts of Jugtown could be made into a museum because of well-documented works from early Moore County. Dean Henry Kamphoefner of the North Carolina State College

School of Design felt that there was the possibility of poor management, under which the high quality observed by the Busbees would be difficult to maintain and Jugtown would rapidly deteriorate. Ben Williams and James B. Byrnes of the North Carolina Museum of Art studied the matter and concluded that Jugtown's major contributions were in the realm of ideas, in intangibles, in the art quality represented there.[14]

Interested people [15] continued to explore the possibility of preserving Jugtown for the State. During May and June more trips were made to Jugtown and meetings were held to discuss Jugtown's future. Juliana said, as she had on previous occasions, that she and her husband had looked forward to making a contribution to North Carolina and that they had always hoped the State could make some use of Jugtown when the Busbees were no longer in charge. Supervising Jugtown had become an arduous responsibility, and she felt that she could not continue its operation much longer. However, she was not in a position at that time to make an outright gift of Jugtown to the State but would consult her friends, consider a sales price, and let the group know the amount.[16]

As negotiations continued, several ways that agencies might take over Jugtown were suggested. These included a joint trusteeship under the North Carolina Museum of Art and the North Carolina Department of Archives and History; a council of interested persons from such agencies as the art departments of colleges and universities, the Department of Conservation and Development, the Moore County Historical Association, and the Society for the Preservation of Antiquities.[17]

In September a list of the property at Jugtown and the operating costs was made. These points were noted:

1. The physical plant includes one residence; one small house used for the display of the pottery; storage shed; a shop building used for throwing the pottery; a shelter for the kilns and two kilns. There are several other small buildings on the 14 acres. The residence includes 3 bedrooms; 1 large common room; a sitting room; an eating room; a kitchen and a bath. All of the buildings are of traditional pioneer log construction.

   2. The operating costs per month are approximately the following:

Salary for the Chief Potter	*$350.00*
Fees for help stacking in kilns	*10.00*
Wood for firing kilns	*25.00*
Clay for refinement	*40.00*
Glazers	*60.00*
Rent of one mule	*5.00*

TOTAL OPERATING EXPENSES
PER MONTH   *$690.00* [18] [sic]

Various state agencies were then approached about the possibility of taking over and running Jugtown. No arrangements could be made, however, for a state agency to take over Jugtown immediately. One person who was active in the Jugtown negotiations explained later:

Insofar as I know, the fact that someone [Juliana Busbee] was living on the Jugtown property played no part whatsoever in our thinking regarding the State's taking over that property.

When this matter was up for consideration, no State agency had in its appropriation sufficient funds to take over and maintain Jugtown. That would not have prevented some agency from making a request from the General Assembly, at its next session, for an appropriation for this purpose —but events moved too rapidly for any such procedure.[19]

Formation of Jugtown, Incorporated

Weeks passed. Conditions at Jugtown did not improve. While many had expressed interest, the situation did not change.

In November, 1958, Ben Owen announced he must leave Jugtown January 1 because he had two children to send to college and he needed a steady income, which he had not had in the past year. Also, he felt he should have an assured future at Jugtown if he was to continue working there. Mrs. Busbee told a friend she had willed Jugtown to Ben Owen and did not owe him money, but her lawyer, Ottway Burton of Asheboro, had no knowledge of such a will. Nor would Mr. Burton draw up a will for Mrs. Busbee at that time because she was, in his opinion, not legally capable of executing a Last Will and Testament.[20]

A group of Juliana's friends now joined together to do whatever they could to help Juliana, Ben, and Jugtown.[21] Arrangements were begun to keep Ben Owen on at Jugtown and relieve Juliana of some of her burdens.

These friends of Juliana's, along with others, making a total of fifteen, whom she had selected and whom she called "The Committee," formed a non-stock, non-profit corporation in early December, 1958. On the advice of the Attorney General it was formed as a non-profit organization so that the State could eventually take over Jugtown after Juliana's death.[22] The corporation was formed for the following purposes:

. . . *perpetuating the history and the art of pottery making in North Carolina and in Moore County in particular.*

.   .   .   .

. . . *to continue to preserve the art and the history of handcrafted earthern* [sic] *ware heretofore made famous by the said Juliana Busbee and Jacques Busbee.*[23]

The arrangement would "care for Juliana's needs and hold Jugtown for educational, historic, and craft interests."[24] Mrs. Busbee, who welcomed the idea, signed a deed on December 5, 1958, turning the Jugtown property over to Jugtown, Incorporated.[25]

In order to obviate any future misunderstandings, a quitclaim, together with the charter of Jugtown, Incorporated, was sent in early December to Juliana's closest relative, her sister Mrs. Judd, for her signature and that of her husband. By this quitclaim deed, if signed, the Judds would have signed away any future claim on Jugtown upon the death of Juliana.[26] Because Mrs. Judd was critically ill, her husband delayed replying or returning the deed. Weeks passed.

While waiting for Dr. Judd to return the deed, Jugtown, Incorporated, had its first meeting. On Saturday, December 27, 1958, the group met at Jugtown to have a picnic lunch and to organize. James Hall was made Acting President, pending the registration of the charter; Isabelle Henderson was elected Vice-President; and Ben Williams was made Secretary-

Treasurer.[27] Other incorporators were Mrs. Margaret Williams, Mary and Blackwell Robinson, Evangeline and Burke Davis, Phillips Russell, Miss Meade Seawell, William Bridges, Ben Owen, Woodrow Pruett, Clarence Thompson,[28] Russell Thompson, Cecil Elliott, and John Alcott.[29]

Finally Dr. Judd replied. Before he and Mrs. Judd would sign the quitclaim deed, they requested that the deed stipulate the conditions for the transfer of the property, insuring Juliana's interests. He wrote:

> For years Juliana has wanted Jugtown to be taken over by the State and operated as a memorial to her husband. If she were able I am sure she would love to donate the property to the State. The hard facts are that she has no other means of subsistence than this property.
>
> If she deeds the property to a group or corporation, it seems to us that she should be given in consideration thereof some dependable and specific statement of the considerations of the transfer of the property.[30]

Jugtown, Incorporated, immediately sent a statement to Dr. Judd agreeing that, if the pottery failed to make a living for Mrs. Busbee, Jugtown, Incorporated, would return the property to her trustee, if she had one at that time, or sell it for her benefit at a public sale.[31]

Mrs. Judd was dying and Dr. Judd seemed unable to make any decisions. More weeks passed. Mrs. Judd died without having signed the deed.[32]

Formation of Jacques and Juliana Busbee's Jugtown, Incorporated

Ben Owen had agreed to remain at Jugtown, despite the long delay in making permanent arrangements, so pottery continued to be turned and orders to be filled. Juliana's mind and memory had not improved. Ben now had complete responsibility for operating Jugtown.[33] From outside appearances, calm and order prevailed.

The calm was but a prelude to the storm that broke in March, 1959. Months had gone by, but out of all the plans and meetings to save Jugtown, no concrete solution had materialized.

Then John Maré, a New Yorker who had first visited Jugtown in 1949, appeared on the scene. Mr. Maré, the son of Domingo Maré, a freighter

captain of French and Spanish descent, and Ellena Shephard of Buenos
Aires, was born on October 28, 1914, aboard his father's ship in the Bay
of Montevideo. One of seven children, John Maré grew up on the East
Side of New York City and later moved to Brooklyn.[34] He worked for
several years with a Wall Street law investment firm, Fraser, Speir, Meyer
& Kidder, took courses at New York University, traveled to Europe several
times, and became an art and antique collector. During World War II he
was commissioned lieutenant commander in the Navy. For a while after
the war he and an old friend, Oliver R. Grace, served together as officials
of Southern Seas Steamship Co., Inc., an operator of steamships and
tankers between the United States and Western Europe. Then he and
Grace invested in a radio station in Southern Pines, an interest which he
later sold.[35] In 1950, he established his home in Southern Pines and in
1951 built radio station WAKN in Aiken, South Carolina, which he
operated.[36]

In answer to one of Juliana's pleas for assistance in operating Jugtown,
Mr. Maré offered to join Juliana in a commercial corporation, and she
agreed.[37] A contract was signed between Juliana Busbee and John Maré
on March 2, 1959, under which they agreed to form Jacques and Juliana
Busbee's Jugtown, Incorporated.

Whereas . . . [John Maré] is desirous of doing everything within his
power to assist in the perpetuation of the distinctive character and tradition of "Jugtown" and at the same time carry on the business of manufacturing and selling pottery for a profit;
. . . with the view to accomplishing their common purpose of preserving
"Jugtown" as a business and carrying on the artistry and ideals there
established by Jacques and Juliana Busbee, [they] have agreed to make
this contract.[38]

Upon Juliana's death, the dwelling house was to be "preserved in an
appropriate way as a memorial [39] to Jacques and Juliana Busbee." Mr.
Maré was to pay to Mrs. Busbee $2,400 in advance and $200 each month.[40]

The following day, March 3, Articles of Incorporation of Jacques and
Juliana Busbee's Jugtown, Incorporated, were signed and acknowledged.
The charter was filed in the office of Thad Eure, Secretary of State, on

March 9 and in the Moore County courthouse on March 11. Mrs. Busbee, Mr. Maré, and his attorney, W. Lamont Brown, were the incorporators. Among the purposes for which the corporation was formed were the following:

To engage in the business of manufacturing, distributing, or otherwise disposing of all types of clay pottery.

.   .   .   .

To manufacture, distribute, sell and otherwise dispose of products in related crafts to the pottery industry.[41]

Mrs. Busbee, despite the previous deed on the Jugtown property, signed another to this new corporation on March 11, 1959.[42]

Shortly after Mrs. Judd's death, Jugtown, Incorporated, learned that Jacques and Juliana Busbee's Jugtown, Incorporated, had been formed and that it, too, had received a deed to the Jugtown property. Juliana did not remember signing either deed.[43]

No longer hoping to receive the quitclaim from Dr. Judd, Jugtown, Incorporated, hastened to file its charter. Mrs. Henderson, Ben Williams, and Blackwell Robinson filed the charter for Jugtown, Incorporated, with the Secretary of State on March 12, 1959. This was the same charter which the incorporators had signed in December, 1958, but which they had never filed. Also in March, they registered "for the first time" the Jugtown stamp.[44]

Two corporations were now in existence, each with a signed deed from Juliana Busbee for the Jugtown property. Both were concerned with Juliana's well-being and the continuance of the Jugtown Pottery. The question was which deed was valid, or whether either was valid.

Ben Owen Leaves Jugtown

On March 23, Mrs. W. A. Mahler, Administrative Assistant for the State Literary and Historical Association, sent Mr. Maré background information concerning Jugtown and asked what his plans for Jugtown were:

*It is felt that all parties concerned have much the same interest at heart,
—the care of Mrs. Busbee, the continuance of Jugtown as a North Carolina industry, the maintaining of the quality of the product, and the continuance of the site in its present architectural form. The Department
of Archives and History is interested in the furnishings of the house as
well as in some of the pictures and books. The State Museum of Art is
also interested in these items.*[45]

In his reply to Mrs. Mahler's letter, Mr. Maré wrote:

*In behalf of the corporation, I will be happy (and I'm sure Mrs. Busbee
will also) to have the North Carolina Museum of Art and North Carolina
Department of Archives and History have joint trusteeship of the "Jacques
and Juliana Busbee's Jugtown Museum" (the said dwelling house and its
contents) and to assist me in seeing that quality of Jugtown in all phases
is maintained.*[46]

In April, 1959, Mr. Maré took over his duties as manager. He had
many plans to change and improve Jugtown. More potters were to be
hired, to be trained by Ben Owen; additional kilns were to be built; im-
provements were to be made in the physical plant; production was to be
increased.[47]

Ben Owen did not agree with Mr. Maré on his ideas for Ben's and
Jugtown's future. Also, he was disappointed at being left out of Mrs.
Busbee's deeds. The relationship between Ben and Mr. Busbee had always
been close. Mr. Busbee had been like a father to Ben, teaching him and
working beside him, as together and with pride they made Jugtown Pottery. The Busbees had said that they wanted Ben to have Jugtown when
they were no longer the operators, but no provision for Ben's inheriting
or purchasing it had been made. Ben did not feel that his future under
the new management justified his staying.[48]

On April 17 Ben Owen refused to sign a contract with Mr. Maré and
left Jugtown.[49] For thirty-seven years he had been the Jugtown potter,
and his name had become synonymous with Jugtown Pottery. His contribution to the pottery industry in North Carolina has been recognized

by many authorities in ceramics. Malcolm Watkins, Curator of the Division of Cultural History at the Smithsonian Institution, wrote:

They [the Busbees], in a sense, elevated the workmanship of Ben Owen to an extraordinarily high level without ever destroying or deflecting any of his basic inherited techniques and craftsmanship and approach to ceramic problems. Thus the Busbees and Ben Owen were united in creating Jugtown as a modern symbol of an ancient tradition; but ultimately it was Ben Owen himself and all he represented of an ancient inheritance and an unwavering artistic integrity that were the foundation and reality of Jugtown.

. . . .

I consider Ben Owen's work to be equal to and often superior to most of the folk pottery in this country. His ability to achieve lightness and mobile qualities of line and proportion in an essentially coarse medium has seldom been paralleled.[50]

And so Jugtown was closed. Mrs. Busbee was temporarily a guest of Mr. Maré. The potter's wheel was silent; black smoke no longer rolled from the kilns. A "Closed" sign hung on the entrance to Jugtown.[51]

Lawsuit and the Closing of Jugtown

On April 22, 1959, Jugtown, Incorporated, entered suit in Superior Court requesting nullification of the deed signed by Mrs. Busbee conveying the Jugtown property to John Maré and Jacques and Juliana Busbee's Jugtown, Incorporated. The complaint alleged that the deed held by John Maré was a "fraud" and was "null and void" on the grounds that

John Maré went to the home of the said Juliana Busbee and by undue influence and chicanery obtained an alleged deed . . . . Juliana Busbee did not have mental capacity to sign a deed and she did not realize nor understand that she had signed a former deed . . . .

Jugtown, Incorporated, also charged that John Maré

is attempting to destroy the value of Jugtown with respect to the art of pottery making and has taken over the said property for the pure purpose of making money and capitalizing upon the reputation and name of the Busbee Jugtown Pottery Works.

It requested that a trustee be appointed by the Court "to take over and hold all the property, both real and personal," of Mrs. Busbee until the matter could be decided by the Court.[52] A temporary restraining order was issued to prevent Mr. Maré and his corporation from disposing of any of the Jugtown property. Pending a hearing, no pottery could be made or sold at Jugtown.[53]

The hearing was set for May 9, 1959,[54] in Rockingham, before the Honorable F. Donald Phillips, Judge, Superior Court. At the hearing, affidavits from Juliana's friends, stating changes noted in her behavior, were presented to Judge Phillips. Two statements from doctors were also presented.[55]

Judge Phillips ruled that Jugtown, Incorporated, was not the proper person to bring a suit to have a deed by Mrs. Busbee set aside. It was neither a relative of Mrs. Busbee, nor had it qualified as next friend; therefore, under the law, it could not represent Juliana's interest. If the suit was to be continued, a member of Juliana's family or a next friend must act in Juliana's behalf and must be a coplaintiff with Jugtown, Incorporated, in bringing the suit. Jugtown, Incorporated, was given thirty days to amend its complaint or to appeal to the Supreme Court.[56] In the meantime, the restraining order was to remain in effect.

On May 12, 1959, Mrs. Louise R. Jordan of Tallahassee, Florida, a cousin and one of Juliana's few relatives, petitioned the court that she be appointed next friend "to see that the interest of said Juliana Busbee is protected." [57] The court, finding Mrs. Jordan to be a "proper person" to act as next friend of Mrs. Busbee, ordered that she be appointed next friend "for the purpose of bringing the action in regard to her property." [58]

In the midst of her troubles, Juliana received an honor to brighten her days. The Woman's College of the University of North Carolina had selected her to receive an honorary degree. The degree of Doctor of

Humane Letters was conferred on Mrs. Busbee on May 31, 1959,[59] with the following citation:

JULIANA ROYSTER BUSBEE: internationally recognized ceramist; former Fine Arts Chairman of the North Carolina Federation of Women's Clubs; charter member and vice-president of the State Art Society; honorary life member of the State Literary and Historical Society; a native daughter who has taken the good earth of her state and shaped it into a thing of beauty; creator, along with her husband, of the pottery which has gained international renown as Jugtown and of the artistic and intellectual mecca called Jugtown which today connotes a way of life, an idea; notable for your expression of basic, creative truths, founded on the highest form of professional discipline; outstanding for your preservation of the extraordinary standard of quality of Jugtown pottery; leading spirit in the revival of the unique crafts of this region; and invaluable contributor to the knowledge and practice of the best of the potter's craft in our time.[60]

Mrs. Busbee, who was now past eighty, once wrote that her only contribution to Jugtown had been "to brag about the pottery . . . and to have the shop in New York where the pottery was introduced." [61] However, friends of the Busbees and visitors to Jugtown knew that much of the charm, beauty, and tradition of the setting was due to Juliana. One native of the Steeds area paid Mrs. Busbee the compliment of saying that she had done "right smart" for their community.[62]

Immediately after the degree was given to Mrs. Busbee, the litigation was resumed. Mrs. Jordan, as next friend of Juliana Busbee, and Jugtown, Incorporated, filed a new suit against John Maré and Jacques and Juliana Busbee's Jugtown, Incorporated, and on June 1, 1959, in open court at Asheboro, Judge W. Reid Thompson of the Superior Court issued a temporary restraining order preventing the defendants from disposing of the Jugtown property and from operating as a pottery. The defendants were given until June 20 to show cause why the restraining order should not be made permanent.[63] A judgment of nonsuit was entered in the first suit.[64]

On June 13, Juliana filed a petition and motion to the effect that the action instituted by Mrs. Louise R. Jordan was "without the authority, knowledge or consent of your Petitioner [Mrs. Busbee]," and that "petitioner, to her best knowledge does not know Mrs. Louise R. Jordan." [65]

The incorporators of Jugtown, Incorporated, then decided that many of their difficulties had arisen from their "reluctance to subject Mrs. Busbee to a competency hearing." [66] If they were to continue with the case, they must have the hearing. A hearing was arranged.

On July 30, Juliana was found to be incompetent "from want of understanding to manage her affairs by reason of mental weakness, age, or disease of old age." [67]

On August 5, 1959, P. H. Wilson of Carthage, North Carolina, was appointed Guardian for Juliana.[68] On August 10, by a consent order, Mr. Wilson was substituted for Mrs. Jordan as a party plaintiff. He was allowed until August 15 to adopt the complaint previously filed by the plaintiffs (Jugtown, Incorporated, and Mrs. Jordan) or to file an amended or a new complaint. The court ordered that the restraining order should remain in effect.[69]

Juliana continued to live at Jugtown while the ownership of the property was being litigated. The legal battle grew between the two corporations.

However, P. H. Wilson, Juliana's Guardian, did not adopt the complaint or file a new one, and on November 16, 1959, the attorney for the defendants submitted a motion to dissolve the temporary restraining order.[70]

Court Decision and the Reopening of Jugtown

The suit was finally concluded on December 8, 1959, when a defense demurrer was sustained and the injunction that had been in effect since June, preventing the production and sale of pottery at Jugtown, was dissolved. The Jugtown Pottery was left in the hands of Jacques and Juliana Busbee's Jugtown, Incorporated, with Juliana as President and John Maré as Vice President and general manager. The judgment was made on the grounds that

. . . Plaintiffs do not have the legal capacity to sue and maintain this Action; . . . Complaint does not set forth facts sufficient to constitute a cause of action against these Defendants . . .

. . . Plaintiffs can neither be benefited nor injured by any Judgment entered by the Court herein;

. . . Plaintiffs have no legal interest in the subject matter of the litigation;

. . . Complaint does not make out even a prima facie showing of the rights of Plaintiffs to have the relief demanded in the Complaint.[71]

Mrs. Busbee is reported to have said, "I am delighted Jugtown will live again. It has been so hard to disappoint so many people." [72]

In March, 1960, the court confirmed the contract made by Mr. Maré with Mrs. Busbee on March 2, 1959, thus ending a year-long litigation over the ownership and operation of Jugtown. Judge Phillips signed the order "in the best interest of Mrs. Busbee," on recommendation of her guardian, Mr. Wilson.[73]

During the year in which Jugtown had been closed, Ben Owen had set up his own shop two miles from Jugtown and was turning the same type of ware he had made for thirty-seven years at Jugtown. His business grew rapidly, for his fame as the Jugtown potter had been established.

Jugtown resumed operations around April 1, 1960, with new potters, new management, and new kilns. Vernon Owens, the son of Melvin Owens, a potter, was now the potter; Charles Moore did the glazing; and Bobby Owens mixed the clay and fired the kiln.[74]

The physical plant was improved and added to by Mr. Maré. The old kilns were rebuilt, two full-sized kilns were added, and a small experimental kiln was built but later torn down. The sales cabin was enlarged and an additional cabin was built.[75]

Mrs. Busbee continued to live in her log cabin and greet visitors. Although her thoughts dwelt in the past and she was forgetful, she continued to charm visitors with her gentle ways and an occasional keen remark.

On March 2, 1962, Mrs. Busbee died at the age of eighty-five at her

fig. 4   JULIANA BUSBEE STANDING IN FRONT OF THE SALES CABIN

home at Jugtown, the place she loved. An editorial in the *Greensboro Daily News*, quoting Valerie Nicholson, paid tribute to Juliana:

"Firelight from the open fireplace and candles in tall holders of orange-colored Jugtown pottery flickered on the old brasses, the dark woods and orange curtains where she extended hospitality to all comers for more than 40 years. For this occasion [a memorial service held for her in the living room of her cabin], it was decorated with the spring flowers she loved.

"The kick-wheel where the pottery is artfully fashioned with the fingers, and the old wood-burning kilns, were stilled for the service, as Jugtown workers paid their tribute to a unique lady. Snowflakes fell on blossoming yellowbells and flowering quince in the yard where her ashes were scattered."

The editorial went on to say:

. . . She had lived in cosmopolitan places around the world; her account of her Greenwich Village days had an unworldly quality in later years— coming from a delicate old lady, her neck encased in delicate lace, a glass of sherry in her hand. One remembers her, vivid and charming, seated on the edge of an old fireplace in an antique house, regaling a dinner party.

Now the two who created Jugtown are gone, but their beautiful creations, like the flowers they planted at Jugtown, live on.[76]

The shadow of death hung over Jugtown. Early in June, only four months after Juliana Busbee had died, John Maré learned that he had cancer. Treatments for the dread disease were unsuccessful, and on August 13, 1962, Mr. Maré died, his life cut short, his plans for restoring Jugtown as a memorial to the Busbees incomplete.[77]

Mr. Maré was a man toward whom friends of Jugtown had mixed feelings. Some felt that he was a godsend to Juliana in her time of trouble and need. He was kind to Juliana and sought to make her last days peaceful and free from worry. He put time and money into the pottery operations, working to reproduce all the old Jugtown designs and to increase the production and sale of the pottery.

On the other hand, Mr. Maré was criticized by many of Juliana's oldest friends for taking advantage of her at a time when her mind and memory were failing. The changes made by Mr. Maré in the physical setting—the building of new kilns, the adding of cabins, signs, picnic tables—were thought to make Jugtown "commercial," and his attempts to increase the production and sale of the pottery were criticized as contrary to the Busbees' philosophy of producing a small quantity of well-made wares.

In his will, Mr. Maré named Oliver R. Grace, his boyhood friend now an executive in a New York investment firm,[78] and Howard C. Broughton, a Southern Pines lawyer, as executors of his estate, with unusually broad powers. They were to hold and manage his business interests

with full authority to sell, settle, and discontinue any of them, at such time or times within the period of twenty (20) years following the date of qualification of my Executors, upon such terms and conditions which, in the sole judgment of my Executors[,] is for the best interest of my estate.[79]

Special attention was called to Jugtown:

. . . I am expecially [sic] interested in the continuation and promotion of Jacques and Juliana Busbee's Jugtown, Inc., and I urge, but do not direct, that my Executors see to the perpetuation of the purposes of said corporation as referred to in the Articles of Incorporation of said corporation. It is my wish that if a sale of said corporation is effected, that the successors will be some person, corporation, or foundation that will continue in the pursuit of the craft of pottery promotion, preserving the folkcraft in a manner that will be a credit to Jugtown, Moore County, North Carolina, and to the spirit of Juliana Busbee.[80]

In accordance with Mr. Maré's will, pottery continues to be made and sold at Jugtown. The staff who have worked there since 1960 carry on the business.

How long pottery will be made and stamped "Jugtown Pottery" is not known. The executors, empowered with the authority to dispose of Jugtown, are faced with the task of deciding what to do with this folkcraft industry, a business which for so many years has been of statewide—and national—interest. They can allow some individual, association, or foundation to take over the corporation, if the proper person or group is found, or, if this is not possible, they can close Jugtown.

FOUR

Recognition Given Jugtown Pottery

Museum Collections

Statements were made by the Busbees [1] and by the press [2] that museums and art collectors all over the United States were interested in Jugtown Pottery [3] and that it had been exhibited in several large museums. [4]

Museums that were named as having had Jugtown Pottery on past exhibit or in their permanent collections were written to to find out if they actually did have this pottery in their collections or if it had been on exhibit in the past. More museums replied negatively than positively—that they did not own Jugtown Pottery nor had they exhibited it in the past. Six museums have been found to have Jugtown Pottery in their permanent collections. Three of these museums are in North Carolina, one is in South Carolina, one is in Ohio, and one is a national museum (Table I). More museums may have owned or exhibited pieces of Jugtown Pottery during the past forty years, but they now have no record of it. The records kept by museums may be inconclusive or incorrect, and pieces that were formerly on display may have been discarded, lost, or broken.

TABLE I

COLLECTIONS OF JUGTOWN POTTERY BY MUSEUMS IN THE UNITED STATES

Museum	Approximate Number of Pieces
The William Hayes Ackland Memorial Art Center [5] University of North Carolina Chapel Hill, North Carolina	1
The Charleston Museum [6] Charleston 16, South Carolina	20
The Cleveland Museum of Art Extension Exhibition Department [7] 11150 East Boulevard at University Circle Cleveland 6, Ohio	12
The Greenville Art Center [8] 802 Evans Street Greenville, North Carolina	30
The North Carolina Museum of Art [9] The Jacques Busbee Memorial Collection Raleigh, North Carolina	100
Smithsonian Institution [10] United States National Museum Washington 25, District of Columbia	3

Exhibits and Lectures

Other museums have had Jugtown Pottery on exhibit, but it is not a part of their present collections. The pottery has also been on exhibit at institutions, for special groups and meetings, and at regional, national, and international craft and trade fairs. The story of Jugtown has been presented through lectures to many groups, clubs, and organizations, but most frequently to women's clubs and school children (Table II).

Sales

The breadth of the recognition given to Jugtown Pottery cannot be estimated from the number of collections in museums or through exhibits and lectures alone. The fame of Jugtown has been spread more frequently by sales and repeat sales to individuals—locally, nationally, and internationally. As early as 1929 the pottery had been shipped throughout the entire Union, "to England, France, Hawaii, all over the States and to Canada, New Zealand, Australia, and Brazil." [11] In 1941, the pottery could be purchased in art and specialty shops in New York City, Philadelphia, Boston, Williamsburg, Nashville, San Francisco, Los Angeles, and Chicago. [12] An order book recording pottery orders in 1950 showed shipments going to all sections of the United States, from East to West, from North to South. [13] When a customer asked if they shipped the pottery, Juliana would answer, "Yes, in a small way we ship all over the world." [14]

TABLE II

EXHIBITS AND LECTURES FEATURING JUGTOWN POTTERY

Date	Event and Location
May 11-23, 1925	Southern Exposition in Grand Central Palace, New York, New York, sponsored by fourteen Southern states to show what progress had been made by the South in arts, crafts, and industry. [15]
—————	Jugtown Pottery and furnishings used for the Broadway show, *Sun Up*, supplied by the Village Store. [16]
Feb. 13, 1928	Exhibit of Jugtown Pottery for Playmakers; lecture by Jacques and Juliana Busbee; demonstra-

TABLE II—(Continued)

Date	Event and Location
	tion by their two potters. Playmaker Theatre, University of North Carolina, Chapel Hill, N.C.[17]
Mar. 4, 1928	Talk by A. F. Greaves-Walker of the Department of Ceramic Engineering, North Carolina State College, to the Mt. Airy [N.C.] Woman's Club on "Where is Jugtown and What is Jugtown Pottery?" [18]
Dec. 6, 1928	Talk by Jacques Busbee at the Suffolk [Virginia] Woman's Club Open House.[19]
Feb. 19, 1930	Program by the Dixie Chapter, the United Daughters of the Confederacy, Columbus, Ohio.[20]
Aug., 1930	Display, Lee Plaza Hotel, Detroit, Mich.[21]
Sept., 1930	Illustrated talk by Caroline Kimball to children of Sunset School, Carmel, Calif.[22]
Jan. 27, 1931	Art Club exhibit in a private home (Mrs. E. L. Gay), Pawhuska, Oklahoma.[23]
July 10, 1931	Three lectures by Mrs. Busbee to University of North Carolina students, with demonstrations of pottery being turned on the kick wheel.[24]
Apr. 20-21, 1934	Demonstration by Ben Owen of turning pottery. Dogwood Festival, Chapel Hill, N. C.[25]
May 16-17, 1935	Exhibit at Binyon Garden [Mrs. Caroline Bean Binyon], for Garden Tour, Georgetown, Washington, D. C.[26]
Spring, 1937	Featured as banquet decorations at the Annual Convention of the Southeastern Arts Association, held in Raleigh, N. C.[27]

TABLE II—(Continued)

Date	Event and Location
Nov., 1937	A National Exhibition of Rural Arts, organized for the Department of Agriculture, Washington, D. C.[28]
Jan., 1940	Exhibit of Contemporary American Ceramics and Batiks, Mint Museum of Art, Charlotte, N. C.[29]
Mar. 1-31, 1940	Exhibition at the Howard University Gallery of Art, Washington, D. C.[30]
Feb. 11–Mar. 19, 1944	Exhibit, "Contemporary American Crafts," Baltimore Museum of Art.[31]
Early 1940's	Talk by Mrs. Busbee and exhibit at Bennett College, Greensboro, N. C.[32]
Nov. 30–Dec. 23, 1947	Memorial Exhibition to Jacques Busbee, Person Hall, University of North Carolina, Chapel Hill, N. C.[33]
Oct. 20-22, 1949	Exhibit at Junior Woman's Club Antique Show, Raleigh, N. C.[34]
Nov. 30, 1949	Talk by Mrs. Busbee on "Jugtown Pottery" to the North Carolina State Art Society at its annual meeting, Raleigh, N. C.[35]
Dec. 1, 1950–Jan. 30, 1951	"The Jacques Busbee Memorial Collection of Jugtown Pottery," State Art Gallery, Raleigh, N. C.[36]
Jan. 25, 1951	Display of The Jacques Busbee Memorial Collection at an Open House in honor of the 1951 North Carolina General Assembly and their families.[37]

TABLE II—(Continued)

Date	Event and Location
May 15-27, 1951	University of Virginia Museum of Fine Arts, Charlottesville, Va.[38]
May 21-31, 1954	Exhibit in the library at Catawba College, Salisbury, N. C.[39]
June 1-20, 1955	Display used in a house furnished by and photographed for use in *House Beautiful*, then house and furnishings shipped to the International Samples Fair, Barcelona, Spain. Exhibition to be shown later in Bari, Italy; Paris; Bangkok; and other cities where the Trade Fairs were held.[40]
April, 1959	Exhibit at Carolina Art Sales Gallery, Raleigh, N. C.[41]
———————	Craftsman's Fair, Asheville, N. C.[42]
———————	Jugtown Pottery included in slide presentation on North Carolina Pottery. Shown to school children in North Carolina, through the Hall of History, Raleigh, N. C.[43]
Nov. 26, 1961	Jugtown featured on the radio program "Profile" over Station WPTF, Raleigh. The pottery received a "Profile Award" from WPTF and the North Carolina Blue Cross Plan, Hospital Care Association, of Durham, for its contribution to the industrial development of North Carolina.[44]
April 1-24, 1962	Exhibit of pottery covering a 35-year period at Salem College, Winston-Salem, North Carolina. The collection, entitled "Jugtown Retrospect," was loaned by Mrs. Mamie Braddy.[45]

Written Recognition

From the beginning of the Jugtown movement up to the present time, Jugtown Pottery has received publicity from the press. Many newspapers and magazines found Jugtown a popular subject because it was a different, interesting story of a folkcraft.

First the New York papers, attracted by the Village Store, carried articles about the quaint, homespun shop; Mrs. Busbee; the North Carolina handicrafts; and especially the pottery. In 1919, the *New York Tribune* called the Village Store "A One Hundred Per Cent American Shop" and announced that the Metropolitan Museum was "soon to give an exhibition of the pottery." [46]

In the early 1920's, national magazines as well as New York newspapers carried stories about this unusual folkcraft pottery from North Carolina. *The Garden Magazine* in 1923 pictured Jugtown Pottery and said:

Beautifully simple and shaped for service, these jars and vases in tones of orange, olive green, brown, and silver-gray seem particularly appropriate for garden and veranda.[47]

By 1923 the name "Jugtown" was familiar to many New Yorkers, but few North Carolinians knew that Jugtown or Jugtown Pottery existed. One North Carolina writer jostled her mother state for not recognizing the pottery that was winning fame in the North:

A few years ago, Jugtown Pottery was as unknown and as unappreciated in New York as, generally speaking, it still is in North Carolina. Today there is in this country no important exhibition of art which does not reserve an honored place for the work of these humble Carolinians. We find great museums and private collectors competing for choice examples of Jugtown Pottery.[48]

The pottery was even becoming known abroad. At a tea given in London, the hostess showed the Jugtown mark on the bottom of the pieces of the tea service. This led to a reporter's assignment to call on all the well-known potteries in the United States.

I decided to first feature the Jugtown pottery, as all the authorities on pottery in New York seemed to think that was the only surviving folkcraft in this country uninfluenced by Europe since 1780. The exhibits of this pottery in New York City were so charming in shape—in color— so simple in effect and so unaffected, that I was fired with the desire to

*get to the place where it was made and to do my article from the produc-
tion end, rather than from the interesting and artistic shop where it has
been so delightfully and informally introduced by Juliana Busbee, and
to verify for myself the interesting tales told in New York about Jugtown
activities and about the two Busbees who seemed to be so intimately
associated with the work.*[49]

By the mid-'20's a few North Carolina papers and journals were carrying articles on Jugtown, but state interest was only slightly aroused.
Gradually, with the growth and popularity of Jugtown Pottery, the pottery
industry in the State grew and other potteries gained publicity. Yet, Jugtown remained a favorite with the press. A local paper praised Jugtown:

*Jugtown pottery emphasizes pottery as an art as contrasted to pottery as
an industry. It is the revival of an old American folkcraft—the only
American folkcraft.*[50]

An extensive study of rural handicrafts in the Southern Highlands
cited Jugtown for contributing to the native pottery of that region:

*Perhaps the product generally known to the public from the Piedmont
section of North Carolina is the Jugtown Pottery, which has been revived
and improved under the direction of Mr. and Mrs. Jacques Busbee. . . . A
few forms of exceptional interest to the student of ceramics and to artist
and collector, inspired by old Chinese influences, have been developed
by the Busbees; but it is the native pottery which is best known, and it is
this traditional product which they have made available through innumer-
able outlets the country over.*[51]

A Philadelphia newspaper wrote of Jugtown's influence on other Carolina potteries:

*Jugtown pottery has become so popular that along the roadside in North
Carolina you can buy all kinds of gaily colored ware, much of it made in
manufactories.*[52]

Charles Grueby, who did tiles at the Cathedral of St. John the Divine,
is reported to have said of the Jugtown Pottery and its creator:

North Carolina natives may have made it. But some talented artist must have planned it. It is even greater in its concept and design than in its execution.[53]

In the '40's and '50's, Jugtown and the Busbees were well known to many people, and their story continued to be popular. Contributors to *The American Home* commented:

Jacques Busbee is the genius behind this Jugtown Pottery of exceptional beauty, color, and individuality. . . . [he] urges his assistants to take their time, to treat each jug or jar as a masterpiece.[54]

An article in the *Ford Times* said:

. . . among artists and designers the small circular stamp marking each piece has become a trademark of good design and fine workmanship.[55]

Jugtown Pottery reportedly even found its way into Presidential quarters. One writer mentioned in 1940 that Mrs. Calvin Coolidge was "one of the many owners of complete Jugtown table services."[56] However, her son, John Coolidge, was unable to locate the pottery among his mother's possessions.[57]

President John F. Kennedy was presented with a pair of black candlesticks in March, 1959, when, as a senator, he spoke at a banquet of the North Carolina Democratic Club in Washington.[58]

President-elect and Mrs. Jack Kennedy are the proud owners of a pair of Jugtown candlesticks, which "Jack was delighted to receive as a gift from this district," it was revealed by Eighth District Congressman A. Paul Kitchin on a visit here this week.[59]

In February, 1962, after over forty years of publicity, Jugtown Pottery, under new management, was once again making a bid for recognition. The Sunday edition of a Southern newspaper carried a full-page coverage of this folkcraft pottery:

. . . the pottery still is being fired in the traditional manner, and some of the old forms which had lapsed through the years have been revived.[60]

Appraisal by Authorities in the Art Field

Many leaders in the art field have recognized Jugtown Pottery for raising the quality of folk pottery to a high level and for being the forerunner in reviving the folkcraft pottery of North Carolina.

One authority on handicrafts, the late Allen H. Eaton, ranked Jugtown Pottery "very high" among the rural potteries of our country for two reasons:

First it was a continuation of the old rural pottery of the South East employing the traditional methods, materials and glazes that had been in use for generations in that area. Secondly Mr. Busbee[,] an unusual artist[,] developed on his own pieces that were reminiscent of Chinese pottery. . . .

It was the Jugtown Pottery which pioneered the introduction of the Southern Highland potteries in the New York and other areas.[61]

Doris E. Dunlavy, head of an art education group at the Cleveland Museum of Art, wrote that the main interest of this pottery lay

in the historical development of small potteries in the United States. . . . It is a "homecraft" type of pottery usually sound in basic design and crafts-manship, perhaps rather better than some of the pottery from these small potteries.[62]

Ben F. Williams, Curator, North Carolina Museum of Art, wrote that the "standard of excellent art quality . . . has made 'Jugtown' stand-out far and above the other potteries of North Carolina."[63]

Bernard Leach, a leading English ceramist, while lecturing in the United States, was asked where he had seen the "last bit of honest folk art" in America. He answered, "Jug Town, North Carolina. I'd known of it 10 years ago. I have examples of it. That was, I think, the last wag of the tail of folk crafts in America."[64]

Mr. Leach also wrote:

I think Mrs. Busbee & her husband did something valuable in helping to preserve & continue a last remnant of American folk pottery, keeping it simple[,] honest & plain. We enjoy using their undecorated redware plates every day—plates that speak of natural clay & firing & of simple country folk. But folk art is dying all over the world as I have seen with my own eyes and I think its main value is for us individualized craftsmen in giving us a jumping off ground of honesty & modesty & technique.

With industrialism & its equivalent education the rot cannot be stopped. The lesson to be learned, I think, is that practice should come before theory even for us.[65]

C. Malcolm Watkins, Curator at the Smithsonian Institution, feels that Jugtown is of great importance as a historical episode in a long history of pottery-making in Moore County,

a history that is still continuing under Ben Owen's leadership in his own pottery, and that will doubtless continue for a long time.

. . . .

Jugtown is historically important because Mr. and Mrs. Busbee recognized the remarkable survival in the Steeds area of an 18th-century tradition, of which vestiges still survived in 1917 in the work of Rufus Owen. . . . they [the Busbees] not only recognized the tradition, but they also stepped in and saved it, taking measures to reinvigorate it and make it a factor in contemporary life. . . . Encouraged by the Busbees and given new inspiration and new challenges to his already deeply ingrained skills, Ben Owen continued to make the pottery of his ancestors, but with new flair and competence and sensitivity to form.[66]

PART II Composition and Design of Jugtown Pottery

FIVE

Clays

Visual Analyses

In the Piedmont section of North Carolina the occurrence of clays suitable for making pottery has long been recognized. In 1897 a state geologist made chemical and firing tests on clay samples from Montgomery and Richmond counties,[1] and further test work and descriptions on a few deposits were published in 1925.[2]

During the summer of 1950 a study was made by the Division of Mineral Resources of the North Carolina Department of Conservation and Development on the deposits of white residual clays or kaolins in the section of the state referred to as the Volcanic Slate Belt. This belt passes through parts of Richmond, Montgomery, Moore, Harnett, Wake, Johnston, and Nash counties and includes the Jugtown area.[3] The deposits of residual kaolin in this belt have formed through normal chemical weathering of certain highly-sheared rocks. A report on this study gives a general description of some of the physical and chemical properties of the clay in this section:

The kaolins are fine grained, often somewhat blocky, relatively free from excessive grit, and do not generally show a high degree of plasticity. Some are very soft and show little structure, whereas others are quite hard and retain many of the characteristics of the rock from which they were derived. In general the clays have a rather dull appearance, although they occasionally display a slight sheen, possibly indicating the presence of sericite.

The texture is variable, however the grain size is usually small. Some clays are very fine-grained, most of the material passing 200 mesh. Others have a fine-grained groundmass but contain hard angular fragments of feldspar and quartz which average less than 1/16 inch in diameter.

Colors generally range from white to brown, iron oxide being the chief cause of discoloration. Where unstained, the kaolin is a greenish to dead white, however some staining is usually present. The clays may be white, white with brown spots of limonite, white with iron stain along cracks and fractures, light cream with brown streaks, tan, brown, and in some cases blue. The bulk of the material is a light cream or white with brown spots and streaks scattered throughout. Clay from the lower portions of a deposit may contain cubes and modules of pyrite.[4]

One particular deposit, "the old Cagle Gold mine along the western side of Cabin Creek, 1¾ miles west of Robbins, Moore County,"[5] is near Jugtown. The clay from this deposit is described as soft kaolin. It

is fine-grained, light cream to white, and contains some fine grit. In general it is relatively unstained except in the upper portions. The harder semi-weathered material underlying and grading into the kaolin is a light tan to greenish tuff in which the fragments are readily visible. It is relatively soft and has a somewhat greasy appearance, indicating the possibility of sericite being present.[6]

Through the years, clays in the Jugtown area have been used in making pottery. Clays from different deposits in this section are not identical but they have similar properties. Potters found that these clays had the right mineral content for shaping pottery and for withstanding the necessary firing temperatures.

To find out the physical and chemical properties of the clays used at Jugtown, the author went to Ben Owen for samples. From his clay bins, Mr. Owen took four separate samples which were similar to the clays

fig. 5 BOYCE YOW REMOVING CLAY FROM THE PUG MILL

he had used while at Jugtown and which he was using at that time. These four samples of clay, representative of the types Mr. Owen had used during his thirty-seven years at Jugtown, were submitted to Stephen G. Conrad of the North Carolina Division of Mineral Resources for visual inspection and identification.

At Jugtown, two or three clays were usually mixed, rather than one clay being used separately. However, since the proportions and the number of clays mixed varied from week to week at Jugtown, depending on the quality of the clays,[7] the four clay samples were studied separately. Sample 1 was used for earthenware.[8] Samples 2, 3, and 4 were used for stoneware and were mixed in varying amounts.

The following report was given of the four samples:

Sample number one is a light gray color, mottled with a significant percentage of yellowish brown iron oxide. In a dry powdered form the iron oxide thoroughly stains the gray clay and the entire sample takes on a bright yellowish-orange color. When water is added to the dry sample, it becomes very plastic and is relatively free from grit.

Sample number two is light gray in color and contains a small percentage of organic matter, mainly in the form of plant roots. It is very plastic and slightly more gritty than sample number one.

Sample number three is practically the same as number two. The only noticeable difference is that number three is a shade darker in the dry powdered form. It, also, has slightly more grit than sample number one.

Sample number four is, also, gray, but is a shade or two darker than the others. It has a much rougher, or lumpier, texture than two and three and contains more organic matter. It, also, contains noticeable areas of iron oxide stain and is not as plastic.

The above descriptions apply to the general physical properties and appearance of the clays.

Although the samples differ somewhat in physical properties, their mineralogy is very similar. All the samples are composed essentially of two minerals; quartz and a clay of the kaolin group. The quartz occurs as clay size, irregular shaped grains, and a few silt size grains. The clay mincral occurs as somewhat rounded aggregates that are several times larger than the average size quartz grains. Under the polarizing microscope these clay aggregates are reddish brown in color. This coloring is believed to be a limonite stain. The stain obliterates most of the clay minerals' optical properties and a positive identification cannot be made. However, based on its index of refraction the mineral is apparently kaolinite, dickite or nacrite.

Quartz and clay appear to be present in about equal amounts. However, this observation is based on visual inspection and may be off as much as plus or minus 10 percent.[9]

SIX

Forms

Utilitarian Shapes

The designs of pottery made in the Steeds area changed as the life of the community changed. Peter Craven's ware was for domestic use, since stores were distant, travel was difficult, and money for imported china and household ware was scarce. During the Civil War, James Fox aided the Confederate cause by turning medicine jars, dishes, bowls, mugs, and other ware that was needed.

After the War and until the end of the nineteenth century, potters along the old plank road made ware for their own use and some for sale. They made churns, crocks, dishes, pitchers, and other pieces that met their simple needs. But their largest volume of business came not from making household wares but from making jugs for the growing whiskey industry. When the prohibition law went into effect in 1909, pottery-making in the Steeds area suffered. Except for a few, the potters' wheels no longer turned. Many pottery shapes were no longer produced and slowly disappeared as people bought their pottery and china from stores.

Then Jacques Busbee appeared in Moore County, bent on having the folk pottery of his native state produced again. So, the utilitarian shapes that had been made for many years in that area became the first pottery of Jugtown. Authentic pieces of ware that had been made one hundred years before were used as guides to retain the same shapes. The traditional, simple shapes were emphasized, and Mr. Busbee also stressed the importance of form, beauty, and fitness.[1]

The utilitarian ware included

cups, saucers, plates, platters, bowls, jugs, churns, crocks, pie plates, butter jars, cream and sugar dishes, candlesticks, tea sets, stew pans, bean pots, pickle jars, preserve jugs, ring jugs.[2]

During the early years at Jugtown a few pieces of pottery were molded by hand by the Jugtown potters and by some of the women and children in the neighborhood. Orange-colored salt and pepper shakers in the shapes of chickens and salt-glazed ducks with blue wings were molded.[3] A frog-shaped weight with holes to be used in the bottom of a flower vase was made with a green glaze. A long, decorative catfish shape was also molded by hand and glazed in green.[4]

Many of the shapes have remained unchanged from Peter Craven's day to the present; only their use may have changed with the years. Today, many people purchase the handmade plates, pitchers, and other utilitarian pieces not so much for their function as for their simple beauty and individuality.

Translations from the Chinese, Persian, Korean

The New York clientele in the 1920's were not content with just the utilitarian shapes. They wanted some ware that was more decorative. This led to Jugtown Pottery's second type of shapes—the translations from the Chinese, Persian, and Korean. Most of the translations are from Chinese pottery of the Han, T'ang, and Sung Dynasties.[5] These shapes are in the form of more decorative pottery and include bowls, vases, and jars in many shapes and sizes.[6] The lines of these translations were usually elongated, graceful, flowing, gently curved. The shapes were aesthetically satisfying and had an appeal to the sense of touch.

Jacques Busbee wrote that when he turned to the Chinese for translations he was only following a tendency of the native potters.

Perhaps the most amazing thing about this pottery is its close similarity

figs. 6 & 7 SELECTIONS FROM THE JACQUES BUSBEE MEMORIAL COLLECTION OF JUGTOWN POTTERY *fig. 6 (opposite page) top row is utilitarian ware; other rows and fig. 7 show translations influenced by the Chinese, Persians, and Koreans in shape to the pottery of primitive periods in various parts of the earth. These potters make a sorghum syrup jug for the table which is exactly like jars taken from the tombs of the Han Dynasty. . . .*

.   .   .   .

All the classic forms of those great periods seem to flicker through the clay as the turner applies the various processes of opening out his clay, pulling it up, widening it, narrowing it, chipping it to an even thickness, &c, &c [sic]. Then it is borne in upon the observer that Chinese shapes are the logical, nay, almost the inevitable outcome of the process of production on a wheel. It is technique crystalized into art.[7]

Juliana expanded on this explanation for using the Chinese translations. She wrote in 1940:

When other things [besides utilitarian shapes] are done, Mr. Busbee goes to the very early Chinese for form. For he thinks the potters of the Han, the T'ang, [and] the Sung Dynasties worked in much the same way of our backwoods country potter. He has tried to teach beauty of form and line. And color in its relation to form. He believes that Primitiveness is a state of mind—not a point in Time.[8]

One authority who did not approve of Mr. Busbee's efforts to imitate Chinese glazes did not object to his introduction of Chinese shapes.

But the assimilation of Chinese shapes into an otherwise strictly Anglo-American potter's style and technique I find very intriguing, esthetically satisfying, and appropriate. Chinese influences are nothing new to American folk pottery, anyway. . . . The essential thing is that Ben Owen has remained true to his techniques and his sense of what is fitting and right for the materials and methods available to him.[9]

Jacques Busbee stressed design in training Ben Owen and Charlie Teague; he believed that the most important element was form. He wrote:

North Carolina pottery is of no consequence in itself without beauty. Being made of N. C. dirt adds nothing to its value unless it is embodied in the forms of Art. For as a matter of fact the whole of art is form. We call it form in pottery and sculpture: proportion in architecture: good drawing in paintings: feeling or soul in music: style in literature. Pottery without beauty of form cannot be made interesting by color, glaze or decoration. The state may accept it from misplaced pride but the world never will.[10]

Ben Owen, who "tried to follow all the shapes he [Mr. Busbee] wanted," indicated that his teacher would not be content with less than perfection. He "had to have them just right." But Ben did not resent this discipline from someone he considered "an artist—he knew shapes and forms."[11]

Ben Owen, who now stamps his pottery, "Ben Owen, Master Potter," is recognized as an outstanding potter and continues to work for improvement in form. He considers form, or shape, the most important thing about pottery.

If you see what you did a year ago and what you do now you will see an improvement in form. . . . You are striving to improve. If you thought you had done your best you would get careless, you would lose interest.[12]

In his shop two miles from Jugtown, Ben Owen makes pottery of the types and quality he had made at Jugtown. His pottery is appreciated by those people who value the beauty of simple forms and the honest use of materials.

Both the utilitarian wares and the translations from the Oriental gained distinction in design from their simple, well-proportioned shapes and from their interesting colors which complement these shapes. Examples of some of the more popular shapes of Jugtown Pottery developed by Ben Owen under Mr. Busbee's direction are shown in figs. 6, 7.

SEVEN

Surface Finishes

Colors of the Glazes

The colors of Jugtown Pottery are as distinctive as their shapes. A brilliant orange pie dish caught Juliana Busbee's eye in 1915; the same vivid orange attracted attention in New York in the 1920's; and the same bright orange still causes comment today.

When Jacques Busbee went down to the Steeds area, potters were making mainly orange earthenware with a transparent glaze and stoneware with a salt glaze. Also at that time, some green ware, similar to the "Frog-skin" that Jugtown later used, was being made by a man in Chatham County.[1] During the early years a glazed orange and a salt glaze also were used at Jugtown on the utilitarian shapes they then were making. The salt glaze was generally decorated with a design in cobalt blue. In 1922 an article mentioned two kinds of Jugtown ware:

. . . 'red ware' and gray stoneware. Redware is really orange, varied in shades from pumpkin yellow to deepest copper, according to the natural colors of the clays and the amount of firing.[2]

While Jacques Busbee was experimenting with new shapes and was adding many Chinese shapes to his designs, he was also experimenting

Plate I   INTERIOR OF THE BUSBEE CABIN

Plate II   JUGTOWN POTTERY ON DISPLAY IN SALES CABIN

Plate III   JUGTOWN POTTERY IN ORANGE   *Bean pot with lid and two handles, traditional shape, 6¼" x 7"*

Plate IV JUGTOWN POTTERY IN "TOBACCO SPIT" *Deep dish platter with two handles, traditional shape, 2¼" x 13¼"*

Plate V JUGTOWN POTTERY IN ORANGE AND YELLOW *(left to right) Pitcher, traditional shape—orange, 5¼″ x 4½″; pitcher, traditional shape—yellow, 5½″ x 5″*

Plate VI   JUGTOWN POTTERY IN MIRROR BLACK   *(left to right) Candlestick, traditional shape, 13½"; bowl with parallel incised design, Chinese translation, 4" x 7⅛"; candlestick, traditional shape, 12"; compote, Chinese translation, 2⅝" x 4⅞"*

Plate VII   JUGTOWN POTTERY IN WHITE   *Bowl, Chinese translation—fluted edge touched with blue-green glaze, 6″ x 11½″*

Plate VIII JUGTOWN POTTERY IN SALT GLAZE *Pitcher, traditional shape—cobalt blue decoration, 7" x 6¼"*

Plate IX JUGTOWN POTTERY IN "FROGSKIN" *Grueby jar with four handles,*
7⅛" x 6"

Plate X   JUGTOWN POTTERY IN CHINESE BLUE *(left to right) Vase, Chinese translation, 4" x 3"; vase, Chinese translation, 6" x 4¾"*

Plate XI   JUGTOWN POTTERY IN CHINESE BLUE   *Jar with two handles, 12″ x 10″*

Plate XII JUGTOWN POTTERY IN CHINESE BLUE *(left to right) Bowl, Chinese translation, 4″ x 5⅜″; bowl, Chinese translation, 4″ x 5⅞″*

with glazes. He added Mirror black, white, Chinese blue, and "Frogskin," which he used on the Oriental shapes. He also introduced the "Tobacco Spit" that was used on the utilitarian ware.[3]

Each piece of Jugtown ware was handmade, and the firing conditions varied from kiln to kiln and from piece to piece within the kiln. Hence, colors varied slightly from piece to piece in each firing and even more from one firing to the next. A "Tobacco Spit" might be almost orange one time and a dark brown the next.

All the Jugtown Pottery was glazed. The colors of the finished pottery came sometimes from the glazes, sometimes from the clay itself, and sometimes from a combination of the two. The colors of Jugtown Pottery were orange, "Tobacco Spit" (brown), yellow (buff), Mirror black, white, salt glaze (gray), "Frogskin" (green), and Chinese blue (blue-green).[4] While the same color varied slightly in intensity, value, and surface texture on different pieces of pottery, the basic colors had the following general characteristics:

Orange—a middle value[5] and strong intensity. This brilliant orange color came from the clay itself rather than from the glaze. The glaze was of a clear type, transparent with a glossy finish. Orange pottery was generally utilitarian ware. One example is the glazed "orange pie dish" that Juliana Busbee reportedly found in 1915. Plate III shows a bean pot in the orange glazed ware.

Sometimes a slip[6] that turned yellow was used on the orange glazed ware as a decoration.

"Tobacco Spit"—middle to low value, medium intensity, medium to dark orange-brown with black spots or streaks caused by the fusing of the minerals in the glaze.[7] The glaze was glossy in finish, of the same clear type as the orange, but with manganese added. "Tobacco Spit" was used on utilitarian ware. Plate IV shows a large, deep dish platter in this color.

Yellow (buff)—high value, medium to strong intensity. A clear glaze[8] was used over stoneware clay, which gave the yellow color and glossy finish; usually used on the utilitarian ware. In plate V a pitcher in yellow is contrasted with a pitcher in orange.

Mirror black—low value, strong intensity. Made from a prepared glaze, glossy in finish. Plate VI shows a pair of candlesticks, a compote, and a bowl, which Juliana Busbee called an "ice bucket," [9] in Mirror black.

White—high value, weak to strong intensity; sometimes had the hue of other wares burned in the same kiln. Made from a prepared glaze. Used mainly on the Chinese translations. Plate VII shows a large bowl in white. This bowl, a translation from a Chinese shape, has a fluted edge touched with spots of blue-green glaze.

Salt glaze (gray)—high value, medium intensity; ranged from a warm gray to gray-blue. Ordinary table salt thrown into the kiln gives the stoneware a semi-glossy to glossy finish; sometimes rough with an "orange peel" finish. Salt glaze was used mainly on the utilitarian shapes. This was one of the original glazes used in the Jugtown area.

A cobalt blue or a white was used as a decoration on the salt glaze ware. Plate VIII shows a pitcher of traditional shape in the salt glaze with a cobalt blue decoration.

"*Frogskin*" (green)—middle value, medium to strong intensity; a yellow-green varying from a semi-transparent to a glossy opaque finish. An Albany slip[10] glaze was used. "Frogskin" was used mainly on translations from the Chinese. Plate IX shows a vase, called a "Grueby jar," in the "Frogskin."

Chinese blue (blue-green)—middle value, medium to strong intensity; color ranges from a light blue to a deep turquoise blue, with spots of red-violet and is semi-glossy in finish. Used on the Chinese translations. Variations of the blue-green are shown in plates X through XII.

The Chinese blue or blue-green glaze was Jugtown's most prized glaze and, according to one authority, some of the best pieces of Jugtown Pottery, usually the Chinese translations, had the Chinese blue glaze.[11] Mr. Busbee mixed this glaze, and after his death Mrs. Busbee requested that, in memory of her husband, the blue-green glaze not be used on Jugtown Pottery.[12] Ben Owen said the formula for this glaze was known only by Mr. Busbee.[13] Another version of the story is that during and after World War II a necessary ingredient in the blue-green glaze could not be purchased and the Chinese blue could not be made.[14]

From 1947 to 1959, no Jugtown Pottery was made using this glaze. When John Maré became owner of Jugtown, experiments with the blue-green glaze began again.[15] Several days before the death of Mr. Maré the group at Jugtown made a small vase in blue-green which they took to him. He was pleased to see the glaze again made in his kilns.[16]

Since 1947 Ben Owen had been requested to make the blue-green glaze, but out of respect for Mrs. Busbee's wishes he had not done so. Now, in his own shop, he is working to duplicate the "lost" glaze. He has achieved a blue-green similar to that he had made at Jugtown. Pieces in this Chinese blue are eagerly sought by those people who have not forgotten Jugtown's most famous glaze but have not been able to buy it for sixteen years.[17]

Enrichment

While two design elements—the shapes and the colors—distinguish Jugtown Pottery, some of the pottery had a little applied decoration and some a small amount of structural decoration. However, even in these pieces, decoration was secondary to shape and color.

In addition to the basic colors obtained through the color of the clay, the color of the glaze, or a combination of these two, some Jugtown Pottery was enriched by a contrasting color. The basic shapes were also sometimes enriched by structural changes in the ware. Examples of enrichment used on Jugtown Pottery are as follows:

I. *Decoration in a contrasting color*—usually a small amount of decoration applied over or under another glaze
   A. Cobalt blue under salt glaze or on white glaze (plates VII, VIII)
      1. Lining on vases and bowls
      2. Brush strokes
      3. Drippings on bowl or spots of color
   B. White glaze under salt glaze
      1. Dogwood flower on wide bowl (fig. 6)
   C. White glaze or yellow slip in a traditional chicken design under transparent glaze on orange ware (on utilitarian ware)

    D. White glaze, blue-green glaze, or green slip glaze as a thick drip not entirely covering the surface (fig. 6)

    E. Yellow slip under transparent glaze on orange ware

II. *Incised design*—made with a sharp stick or pointed edge (fig. 6, plates VI, VIII)

    A. Band or radial lines around the neck of a Chinese jar

    B. Intertwining linear decoration on pitchers and vases

    C. Parallel lines around a vase or bowl

III. *Applied clay* (fig. 7)

    A. "Ears" of clay

    B. Handles on vases

    C. Ropes of clay, usually on Chinese jars and vases

IV. *Impressions in clay*—made with the fingers

    A. Thumb prints

    B. Parallel indentations (fig. 6)

    C. Fluted edge (plate VII)

EIGHT

Processes

The procedure for making Jugtown Pottery has remained almost un-changed through forty years of operation. The tools and equipment are like those used in pre-Revolutionary times rather than in the twentieth century. Mrs. Busbee wrote of Mr. Busbee's reason for bypassing modern machinery and mass production:

My husband's object has always been to have this pottery a studio out-put. He believed that handcraft should be lovingly, sparingly done. That the workers should be accounted artists, and that the unceasing effort for beauty should bring, from within, the life abundant. A factory output has never interested him. It is not how much that is done but how beauti-fully and the work should never be drudgery. When a very beautiful thing is done—then—a Roman Holiday! [1]

Preparing Clay

The first step in making Jugtown Pottery was to obtain a supply of the raw material—clay. Ben Owen, Mr. Busbee, or some men in the neighbor-hood went to a clay bed in the surrounding area of Moore, Randolph, and Montgomery counties and dug the clay. Clay was usually dug from a

fig. 8   KICK WHEEL AT JUGTOWN

wooded area, the bank of a field, a dried-up river or pond bed, or the bottom of a swamp. Picks, axes, and shovels were needed to loosen the clay, which was often as hard as stone. The clay was loaded on a wagon in the early years, later on a truck,[2] and hauled to Jugtown.

The dry clay was first put into bins. During the early years at Jugtown, the clay was put into a pug mill, an ancient type of machine used for grinding and mixing the clay.[3] One or two mules were kept for turning the mill. For the last twenty years a mule was rented about once a week.[4] In 1948, the rent for the mule was noted as $5 a month.[5] The pug mill had a long wooden timber which protruded from a round, tub-like container holding the clay, and as the mule, hitched to the timber, went round and round, wooden mixing blades crushed the clay.[6] Water was then added to clay powder and mixed in the pug mill. (fig. 5)

The clay was then put into a pit dug in the ground inside the pottery shed and covered to keep it from drying out. Enough clay was mixed for about two weeks' work. Clay was taken from the pit as it was needed.

In digging the clay, they tried to get clay that was as free from roots and foreign materials as possible. During the years Mr. Busbee was living these imperfections were not screened from the clay powder before it was ground in the pug mill. Instead, Ben Owen "picked" his clay clean after it had been mixed with water. This was done by drawing a wire through the moist clay, cutting off "sheets" of clay that exposed the rough, unwanted foreign particles. After about 1957 or 1958, the clay that had been ground to a powder was sifted through a screen sieve and was then put into the pug mill and mixed with water. The sieve removed most of the roots and small grit particles, and Ben removed the remaining imperfections by cutting through the clay with the wire.[7]

The amount of clay needed to make a particular piece of pottery was determined on a set of homemade scales. Although the scales actually weighed the clay in pounds and ounces, the potter judged the amount of clay in gallons—a term he understood to refer to the size of the object to be made. For example, a ball of clay "weighing" one gallon was the amount needed to make a one-gallon jug.[8]

After water had been added and the clay had been cleaned, it had to be

fig. 9   THE KILN (foreground) AND BEN OWEN COMING FROM THE CABIN WHERE HE MADE POTTERY

kneaded, like dough, to remove all air bubbles which would have caused blisters or cracks in the finished piece of ware. After the clay had been kneaded, it was ready for use.

Turning

Now comes the true test of a skilled potter—to turn a formless mass of clay into a shape of beauty and of good proportion. The clay is centered and thrown on a "kick wheel," a circular head which is turned by kicking a lever. (fig. 8) As the lump of clay turns on the wheel, the potter shapes it with his hands. As he works, he puts some water on the clay to keep it from sticking to his hands. He drops his thumbs down to make an indentation; the clay opens up. He draws the clay up, shaping it with one hand on the inside, one hand on the outside. In a matter of minutes the clay takes the shape of a jug, a vase, or a candlestick. When the piece is finished, a wire is drawn under the bottom to loosen it from the wheel head. Then it is set on a board rack to dry before being fired. The length of time necessary to air dry the ware depends partly on the weather, but usually the small pieces of pottery, such as cups, saucers, and small vases, must dry for four or five days. Larger pieces, such as candlesticks or large jugs, take a week to dry.[9] When the ware is sufficiently dry to handle, but not yet hard, a stamp is pressed into the bottom of the ware, marking it "Jugtown Pottery."

Stoneware pieces which are fired only once are decorated before being placed in the kiln. The other ware is first fired unglazed, then glazed and refired.

Glazing

Applying the glaze to the pottery was Mr. Busbee's chosen job when he lived. Mr. Owen mixed the glazes, with the exception of a special blue-green glaze, the formula for which Mr. Busbee alone knew. The glazes were applied by dipping or painting. After Mr. Busbee's death, Mrs. Busbee did some of the glazing; however, Mr. Owen took over most of the mixing and glazing.[10]

fig. 10   BEN OWEN CHECKING POTTERY BEFORE PUTTING IT INTO THE KILN

Firing

When enough pieces of ware were dry, they were stacked in the ground-hog kiln for firing. The groundhog kiln was a horizontal brick flue embedded in the ground with its top slightly above the surface. A fire was built at the front end, and the chimney rose about six to eight feet at the other end. The pottery was stacked in the center section, between the fire and the chimney. The center section of the kiln was raised to about one-half the height of the kiln. Ground flint was scattered over the dirt so that the high-fired stoneware would not rest directly on the ground and the heat would circulate to all parts of the ware. Some of the earthenware and larger pieces of stoneware were placed on trivets, usually called stilts.[11]

Mr. Busbee wrote about the confusion he had noted in stacking the kilns:

The smaller children are nicknamed "stackdoodles" for stacking a kiln bears a strong resemblance to an old time bucket company at a village fire. The potter crawls into the kiln and begins to stack at the upper end, so that two are required inside the kiln to hand the ware up to him and two on the outside to hand it in. The stacking of the kiln is confusion—the potter inside shouting for ware that has not been brought from the shop, the "stackdoodles" getting in each other's way, breaking off handles and violently disclaiming the accident, or leaving the job entirely to run to the house for a biscuit or a cold sweet potato. The whole affair is a very temperamental proceeding.[12]

There were originally two kilns at Jugtown, one for stoneware and one for earthenware. After Mr. Maré became manager at Jugtown he had the old kilns, which were in need of repair, rebuilt; two full-sized kilns were added; and a small experimental kiln was built but later torn down.[13]

The stoneware, which was unglazed when it went into the kiln, was fired only once at a high temperature—2300°-2400°F.—for about fourteen hours. White and green ware were fired together in the stoneware kiln for ten to twelve hours. After the firing, the kiln was cooled for three days and then the ware was removed from the kiln.[14]

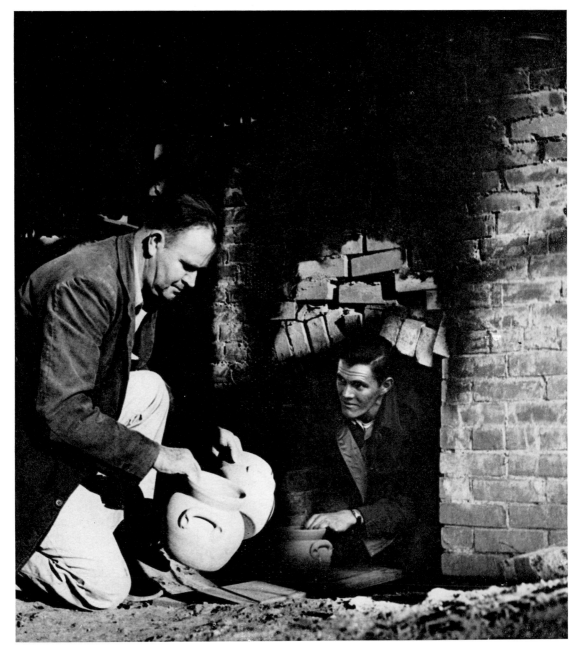

fig. 11   BEN OWEN (left) AND CHARLES MOORE STACKING BEAN POTS IN THE GROUNDHOG KILN

The earthenware, which was glazed, had to be fired twice, once before glazing and once after glazing. Both firings were at a lower temperature than that of the high-fired stoneware kiln—1700°-1800°F.—and each firing required eight to ten hours, with a two-day cooling off period after each firing. After the first firing, the unglazed earthenware came out a yellow-orange color and was called bisque. Then it was glazed, returned to the kiln, and refired.[15]

Firing the groundhog kiln was a job that required careful attention by the stoker. Many variables could cause a change in the temperature in the kiln: the amount and type of wood burned, a change in the weather, a strong wind, a cold rain. Firing a kiln too fast or too high could result in the loss of an entire kiln of ware. For this reason, opening the door on each newly-fired kiln of ware was a moment of suspense and anticipation.

The fire was begun slowly with oak logs, heating the ware gradually to prevent cracking. A sheet of iron was laid over the chimney to keep all the heat in the kiln. The stoneware kiln reached its maximum temperature after about ten to eleven hours; then blasting began. This was near the end of firing; splints of pine were thrown into the kiln, making the fire burn fast and running the flame to the back of the kiln. Pine was burned about two to three hours to maintain a high temperature.[16] Blasting usually started late in the afternoon or shortly after dark. The sheet of iron was removed from the chimney; flames, drawn from the front of the kiln over the pottery to the back and up through the chimney, rushed out, leaping high into the air. Along with the flames, a dense, black smoke mounted from the chimney, rolling and curling several hundred feet into the air, attracting neighbors from miles around.[17] (fig. 12) Against the darkening sky, the smoke and the red-orange flames were a brilliant, colorful contrast.

Immediately after blasting, while the wares were still glowing with an incandescent light, the time had come for salting. Bricks were removed from flue holes in the top of the kiln and handfuls of salt were thrown through the holes. The salt sizzled like fat when it touched the white-hot ware. About two and one-half gallons of salt were thrown into the

fig. 12   A DENSE BLACK SMOKE RISES FROM THE GROUNDHOG KILN DURING FIRING

kiln. The flame now changed to almost white with streaks of blue, green, and red. Then the chimney was covered with a sheet of iron and the kiln was left to cool slowly for three days.[18]

The firing of a kiln was an occasion for a party among the workers at Jugtown. While the kiln was still warm, they often roasted hot dogs over the chimney on pronged sticks. Rolls were warmed on the kiln and slaw and cold drinks were served. Any visitors or neighbors who happened to be around were invited to join the party.[19]

After the kiln had cooled for several days, a group would gather to see the pottery as it was removed from the kiln. The entire process, from freshly-dug clay to the still-warm glazed pottery, had taken many weeks. This process was repeated month after month, year after year, yet the thrill of seeing a kiln of newly-fired pottery never faded.

After the ware had been removed from the kiln and admired, it had to be cleaned, sorted, and inspected. Pieces of flint that had stuck to the bottom of the ware and that were often razor-sharp were polished off with sandpaper. Containers were tested to see if they were waterproof, or "housebroke," as Juliana said.[20] Then came the final inspection. In his lifetime Mr. Busbee was the final critic on the acceptance or rejection of a piece of Jugtown Pottery. If a piece had any tiny imperfection and failed to meet his standards, it would be discarded. When asked what was done with the pieces of discarded pottery, Mrs. Busbee gave a stock answer, "We use them to stop erosion." [21]

Some of the pottery was kept for sale at Jugtown, but most of it was packed into barrels for shipment to out-of-state customers. Jugtown was miles from a paved road, a train station, or a harbor, and shipping the pottery was a problem during the first years. However, even an inconvenience could be a pleasure if approached with the proper attitude:

But on Saturdays were fiesta days! Rain or shine the mule was hitched to the wagon piled high with barrels of pottery for New York and we made an all day trip to Hemp [Robbins—7 to 8 miles away]. In those days it took all day to go to Hemp and back." [22]

PART III Prospect

NINE

The Future of Jugtown

In 1917, when Jacques Busbee arrived at Seagrove, surely he did not anticipate the length of his venture with pottery. He planned to work for only about a year, just long enough to get the industry on its feet. Had he foreseen in his future a life removed from modern conveniences, a country life miles from a highway, where visitors ventured only when weather permitted,[1] he might have given up his early plans.

But he did not give up those plans. His dreams grew and led to larger plans.

Old potters were found, but young potters proved to be even better craftsmen. The best of the old traditional pottery was saved, but a further step was taken. Not only were the wares which had been made in the past century by such families as the Cravens, the Owens, and the Teagues revived, but new shapes and colors were also made. Pie plates and dishes in the traditional bright orange were popular, but collectors sought even more avidly the vases in Chinese blue.

From the crude potters' wheels in a small wooden shed in a little-known section of Moore County came pottery that was simple but beautiful, pottery that was sought for its aesthetic appeal as well as for its use. This pottery, never mass-produced but turned by hand, piece by piece, gradually found its way into exhibits, museums, private collections, and even Presidential quarters.

The shelves at the Jugtown sales cabin were almost continually bared by visitors from all over the United States, people who had read about Jugtown or who had heard from someone else the Jugtown story. The fame of this pottery spread as it was shipped to all parts of the Union—North, South, East, West—and even to many foreign countries.

The publicity which increased over the years cannot be credited solely to the pottery. The planners, the promoters, the adventurers—the Busbees—were constantly at work. Realizing the value of the unusual, the Busbees patterned their life to fit their primitive backwoods setting. Life was simple, but stimulating. Visitors were welcomed with food and drink and an account of their hosts' venture. Their simple log cabin became a haven for intellectuals, artists, politicians. Friends came frequently—to dine, to talk on worldly topics, to relax in the country, to meet friends—and the Jugtown tale spread.

Now the Busbees have died and the Saturday night gatherings of colonels, writers, businessmen, actors, and professors for roast pheasant and stimulating debates have ceased. The peacocks that Mr. Busbee raised no longer roam the yard. A cabin now stands where once his prized iris garden grew.

But the hand of Juliana is still seen in the cabin—in the touch of pine boughs on the hearth, in the familiar orange curtains at the windows. The big straw basket which Juliana had woven still stands as a reminder of the couple who loved native handicrafts.

And in the Jugtown community and in potters' shops over the State the influence of the Busbees and their pottery lives on. Pottery-making has grown to be a large and profitable industry in many sections of the State.

Potters have added new colors and shapes to their lines, and they find a nationwide market for their wares. They, like the Busbees, find quality a good selling point as well as a goal in achieving a personal satisfaction and pride in their craft.

Perhaps the most direct tie to the Busbees' influence is Ben Owen. Today, in his own shop, a simple log cabin with dirt floor, Mr. Owen receives visitors and orders from all over the United States. His hands are now bent with rheumatism, but he continues to shape the same type of ware he has made for over forty years. He is a man respected and loved by many for his humility, his skill, and his fidelity to his craft.

With the death of the Busbees and of John Maré and the absence of Ben Owen, an era has ended at Jugtown. Jacques Busbee cannot appeal to North Carolinians to preserve and continue a folkcraft industry in their native state. Juliana Busbee cannot plead for some state agency or individual to take over Jugtown and make it a memorial to her husband. John Maré might have met the challenge to keep Jugtown in operation, but his untimely death cut short his plans. Ben Owen, so long identified with Jugtown, can no longer stamp his pottery "Jugtown Pottery."

The future of Jugtown remains uncertain. One editor has questioned the soundness of continuing Jugtown. He suggested that the larger question concerning the future of Jugtown is not *would* Jugtown continue but *should* it continue.

With the head [Jacques], heart [Juliana], and hands [Ben] gone, what is really left of Jugtown but a place?

.   .   .   .

Unless there is some strong, compelling personality not only willing to take that chance [of restoring Jugtown] but also capable of drawing people to the place as the Busbees did, it is better that Jugtown, the place, remain alive as a cherished memory—and its products a cherished and rare possession.[2]

Folkcraft pottery in North Carolina again faces a possible crisis. In 1918, the crisis was caused by a lack of demand for utilitarian pottery; today the demand for the simple, hand-crafted pottery exceeds the wares produced. The great problem now is a lack of skilled craftsmen to take

fig. 13   STILTS AND DISCARDED POTTERY IN FRONT OF THE GROUNDHOG KILN

over after Ben Owen and the remaining traditional potters leave their potter's wheels. A reporter recently wrote:

Are the pottery-makers of Moore and Montgomery Counties—who represent generations of craftsmanship—about to pass from the North Carolina scene at a time when the demand for the hand-crafted objects is at a peak?

.   .   .   .

Their problem is manpower, a new generation to carry on a tradition that in some cases extends back 200 years.

.   .   .   .

The glory of the present moment is that so much good utilitarian pottery is being turned out in the area; the pity is that it is so doubtful how much longer any of the potteries can continue in existence.[3]

Only time will tell what the future of Jugtown and of traditional pottery in North Carolina will be. Whatever the future brings, the story of Jugtown Pottery has been a colorful thread in the history of North Carolina and in the history of folkcrafts. Jugtown embodied the pioneer spirit. It encouraged creative living. It struggled to revive pottery-making by traditional methods and to raise the quality of the craft to a high level. It gave to the field of crafts a pottery that was distinctive in shape and color, a pottery that merited being called an American folkcraft.

NOTES TO CHAPTER I

1. Hugh Talmage Lefler and Albert Ray Newsome, *North Carolina: The History of a Southern State* (Chapel Hill: The University of North Carolina Press, 1954), p. 362.

2. [Jacques Busbee], Record Book, MS, n.d., p. 75 (in the files of the late John Maré, Southern Pines, N. C. Mr. Maré was owner of Jugtown from 1959 until his death in August, 1962).

3. "An Isolated Industry: Pottery of North Carolina," *The Journal of Geography*, XXV, No. 6 (September, 1926), 222–23.

4. "A Brief Outline of the Pottery Industry of North Carolina," MS (received from the Department of Ceramic Engineering, North Carolina State College of the University of North Carolina, Raleigh, N. C.), n.d. (in the files of the writer). (Mimeographed.)
Most of the statements about the Cravens are supported by John Ramsay, *American Potters and Pottery* (Clinton, Massachusetts: Hale, Cushman, & Flint, Colonial Press, Inc., 1939), p. 85. However, Mr. Ramsay lists the first potters in North Carolina as the Moravians who settled in North Carolina about 1740 (p. 83). He also gives a chronology of the potters from Steeds, in Moore County (p. 241). [Actually, Steeds is in Montgomery County.]

5. "Demand for Art Pottery Spurs Revival of Craft in Carolina," *News and Observer* (Raleigh), July 7, 1929, p. 8.

6. "Pottery in N. C.," Letter to the Editor, *News and Observer* (Raleigh), July 21, 1929.

7. Ben Dixon MacNeill, "Sandhill Potters Reviving Oldest of Arts in Jugtown," *News and Observer* (Raleigh), April 3, 1927.

8. Adelaide L. Fries (ed.), *Records of the Moravians in North Carolina* ("Publications of the North Carolina Historical Commission," Vol. I,

1752–1771 [Raleigh: Edwards and Broughton Printing Company, State Printers, 1922]), pp. 148–59.

9. A. H. Rice and John Baer Stoudt, *The Shenandoah Pottery* (Strasburg, Virginia: Shenandoah Publishing House, Inc., 1929), p. 7.

10. "Johnson Jug Factory: Catawba County Boasts Original 'Jugtown' Site," *Hickory Daily Record*, U. D. C. Edition, February, 1938. According to this reference, there was a post office at Jugtown in Catawba County which received mail from January 19, 1874, to March 31, 1906.

11. "Peter" and "Pater" are two spellings which writers have used in referring to the same man. "Peter" is the more frequent spelling.

12. M. R. Dunnagan, "Pottery Making, Ancient Art, Increasing in State," *The E. S. C. Quarterly*, V, No. 2–3 (Spring-Summer, 1947), 53.

13. Letter from R. E. Wicker, Pinehurst, N. C., to writer, February 27, 1962.

14. "To the Editor," MS, n.d., p. 2 (in the files of Blackwell P. Robinson, Professor of History, The Woman's College of the University of North Carolina, Greensboro, N. C.).

15. Interview with Mrs. Mamie H. Braddy, a reporter and a long-time friend of the Busbees, Winston-Salem, N. C., June 22, 1962.

16. [Jacques Busbee], Record Book, p. 63.

17. Ethel Stephens Arnett, in her book, *Greensboro, North Carolina: The County Seat of Guilford* (Chapel Hill: The University of North Carolina Press, 1955), p. 450, mentions a John Sloan who was captain of the Guilford Grays and participated in twenty battles during the Civil War.

18. [Jacques Busbee], Record Book, pp. 63–71.

19. A letter to Mr. Busbee, signature missing, says Thomas was not a turner. Clayton, Indiana, 9/25 [*sic*] (in the files of John Maré).

20. "Smalt \smȯlt\ *n* [MF. fr. OIt *smalto*, of Gmc origin; akin to OHG *smelzan* to melt—more

at SMELT]: a deep blue pigment used esp. as a ceramic color and prepared by fusing together silica, potash, and oxide of cobalt and grinding to powder the resultant glass." By permission. From Webster's Seventh New Collegiate Dictionary, copyright 1963 by G. & C. Merriam Co., Publishers of the Merriam-Webster Dictionaries.

21. Record Book, p. 63.

22. Interview with Ben Owen, who turned pottery at Jugtown for thirty-seven years, and Boyce Yow, who fired kilns at Jugtown for several years, February 8, 1962.

23. [Jacques Busbee], Record Book, p. 73.

24. Letter, n.n., n.d. (in the files of John Maré).

25. [Jacques Busbee], Record Book, p. 75.

26. Interviews with Boyce Yow, October 18, 1961, and February 8, 1962.

27. As noted by the writer, October 7, 1961.

28. Ruth Kedzie Wood, "Jugtown, Where They Make Jugs," *The Mentor*, XVI (April, 1928), 36.

29. [Jacques Busbee], "A Colonial Hangover," MS, n.d., p. 8 (in the files of Blackwell P. Robinson).

30. Juliana Busbee, "New Ways for Old Jugs—Art in Jugtown Pottery," *The E. S. C. Quarterly*, V, No. 2–3 (Spring-Summer, 1947), 60.

31. Jacques Busbee, "To the Editor," p. 2.

32. Hugh T. Lefler, *History of North Carolina* (New York: Lewis Historical Publishing Company, Inc., 1956), II, 711. Prohibition was adopted in North Carolina in 1908, became effective in 1909.

33. Juliana Busbee, "Jugtown Pottery: A New Way for Old Jugs," *The Bulletin of the American Ceramic Society*, XVI, No. 10 (October, 1937), 415.

34. Jacques Busbee, "To the Editor," p. 3.

NOTES TO CHAPTER II

1. Jacques Busbee, "To the Editor," p. 7. Mr. and Mrs. Busbee reveled in collecting expressions of local speech and ballads, which they frequently used in their writings and lectures.

2. "Piedmont Pottery," MS from the files of Juliana Busbee, supposedly her work, p. 1 (in the files of Blackwell P. Robinson).

3. Letter, Ben [F. Williams], Curator, North Carolina Museum of Art, Raleigh, N. C., to Blackwell [P. Robinson], January 15, 1959 (in the files of Blackwell P. Robinson).

4. "Busbee Home Will Go Soon," *News and Observer* (Raleigh), October 12, 1914. The article also said, "But the house itself, the dwelling[,] is not all. On the corner is the one-room law office, Supreme Court room, studio and school. Erected as the law office of Judge Wm. Gaston, it was used as the Supreme Court room of N. C. during the time while the State was undergoing erection following the burning of the old one. Here Judge Gaston wrote 'The Old North State' and it was here he died."
Among the Busbees' collections were two hand-written visiting cards: "H. Clay of Ashland. Raleigh. 16 Apr. 1844," and "Raleigh, N. C. March 14 1865. G. T. Beauregard. General." (In the files of John Maré.)

5. R. C. Lawrence, "The Story [of] Jacques Busbee, Poet of Pottery, and of Our Own Jugtown," *Pilot* (Southern Pines and Aberdeen, N. C.), December 15, 1939.

6. Albert Nelson Marquis (ed.), "*Who's Who in America: A Biographical Dictionary of Notable Living Men and Women of the United States,* XIII (Chicago: A. N. Marquis & Company, 1924–25), 603.

7. "Club Lecturers," brochure of programs to be given through the Art Department of the Fed-

eration of Women's Clubs of North Carolina, 1915–1916. Two lectures were scheduled for Mr. Busbee: "Modern Landscape" and "Art in Child Life" (in the files of John Maré).

8. Newspaper article from Hickory, N. C., n.n., April 22, 1911 (in the files of John Maré); "School News," Columbia, S. C., n.d. (in the files of John Maré); Jacques Busbee, "Kill Devil Hill," *The North Carolina Booklet*, XI, No. 2 (Raleigh, N. C.: The North Carolina Society, Daughters of the Revolution, October, 1911), 99–104; Jacques Busbee, "My Great Aunt and 'Carolina,'" *The North Carolina Booklet*, XII, No. 4 (Raleigh, N. C.: The North Carolina Society, Daughters of the Revolution, April, 1913), 211–15; Jacques Busbee, "Tales of the Borough Towns of North Carolina," MSS, n.d. (in the files of Blackwell P. Robinson).

9. Letter, Ben [F. Williams] to Blackwell [P. Robinson], January 15, 1959.

10. Jonathan Daniels, "Tarheel Capital," *Holiday*, XIX, No. 2 (February, 1956), 41. This writer pointed out several prominent Raleigh families. ". . . the distinguished Royster family . . . providing generations of good physicians. They came as skilled Scottish cabinetmakers to furnish the Doric capitol. . . . one of Raleigh's most distinguished physicians was Dr. Wisconsin Illinois Royster. His sister was Virginia Carolina. Iowa Michigan Royster was killed at Gettysburg. And today, Vermont Connecticut Royster (strayed from home) is a Pulitzer prize-winning editor of *The Wall Street Journal*." Reprinted by special permission from *Holiday*, copyright 1956, by The Curtis Publishing Co.

With respect to William Royster, Juliana's father, Vermont Royster wrote: ". . . he was a cousin of my grandfather and the other Roysters with state names and I grew up calling Mrs. Busbee 'Aunt Juliana.'" (Letter, Vermont Royster, Editor, *The Wall Street Journal*, to writer, July 10, 1963.)

11. Letter, Ben [F. Williams], to Blackwell [P. Robinson], January 15, 1959.

12. "Club Lecturers."

13. Jacques Busbee, "To the Editor," p. 1.

14. Mildred Harrington, "Interesting People: The Master Potter of Jugtown," *The American Magazine*, CIII, No. 6 (June, 1927), 72–74.

15. MS on the life of Juliana Busbee (in the files of Blackwell P. Robinson). (Mimeographed.)

16. Juliana Busbee, *The Bulletin of the American Ceramic Society*, p. 418.

17. [Juliana Busbee], MS for talk given to "B. & P. W. C., Winston-Salem, N. C., 1931," pp. 3–4 (in the files of Blackwell P. Robinson).

18. [Juliana Busbee], "For Lawrence of Lumberton," MS, n.d., pp. 1–2 (in the files of Blackwell P. Robinson).

19. Jacques Busbee, "To the Editor," p. 1.

20. *Ibid.*, p. 2.

21. Hatcher P. Story, "Lost N. C. Art is Made to Live Again; Pioneer Craft with a Pedigree: That Would Be Jugtown, U. S. A.," *Charlotte Observer*, December 17, 1950.

22. Mamie H. Braddy, "University Honors Busbee as Master of Pottery Art," *Twin City Sentinel* (Winston-Salem), December 13, 1947, p. 10.

23. Juliana R. Busbee, "Jugtown Comes of Age," *The State*, V, No. 3 (June 19, 1937), 7.

24. [Jacques Busbee], "A Colonial Hangover," p. 2.

25. Juliana R. Busbee, *The Bulletin of the American Ceramic Society*, p. 419.

26. Interview with Boyce Yow, October 18, 1961.

27. Jacques Busbee, "To the Editor," pp. 3-5.

28. Burke Davis, "State Now Taking Note of Its Artistic Pottery; Chinese and Native De-

signs; Jugtown Reclaims an Old Art," *Greensboro Daily News*, February 17, 1952.

29. Juliana R. Busbee, "Age-Old Profession Now Flourishes in Sand Hills," *News and Observer* (Raleigh), June 5, 1927.

30. Juliana Busbee, MS, n.d. (in the files of Blackwell P. Robinson).

31. Jacques Busbee, "To the Editor," p. 5.

32. Jacques Busbee, "Jugtown Pottery," *Ceramic Age* (October, 1929), pp. 127-30.

33. "Piedmont Pottery," p. 2.

34. Letter from R. E. Wicker to writer, February 27, 1962.

35. Interview with Boyce Yow, February 8, 1962.

36. Juliana R. Busbee, "Jugtown Comes of Age," *The State*, p. 7.

37. Jacques Busbee, "To the Editor," p. 6.

38. Juliana Busbee, *The E. S. C. Quarterly*, p. 60.

39. "Jugtown Pottery, An American Folk Craft. A Memorial Exhibition to Jacques Busbee, 1873-1947," brochure for exhibit, Person Hall Art Gallery, University of North Carolina, Chapel Hill, N. C., November 30-December 23 [1947] (in the files of the North Carolina Collection, U. N. C. Library).

40. Interview with Ben Williams, March 22, 1962.

41. Jacques Busbee, "To the Editor," p. 9.

42. MS on the life of Juliana Busbee.

43. Letter, Mrs. Robert M. Duckett, Raleigh, N. C., to writer [July 30, 1962].

44. Elene Foster, "A One Hundred Per Cent American Shop," *New York Tribune*, July 27, 1919.

45. [Juliana Busbee], "B. & P. W. C.," p. 4.

46. Interview with Clarence Thompson, July 17, 1962. Mr. Thompson met the Busbees in 1933 and from that time until two years before Juliana's death was one of their closest friends, spending most holidays and Sundays with them. Mr. Thompson has an outstanding collection of Jugtown Pottery in blue-green.

47. Letter from Mrs. Robert M. Duckett [July 30, 1962].

48. [Juliana Busbee], "B. & P. W. C.," p. 5.

49. Handwritten notes by Clarence Thompson (in the files of the writer).

50. Mildred Harrington, "Village Store is Moore County," *Greensboro Daily News*, n.d. (in the files of John Maré).

51. Interview with Ben Owen, February 8, 1962.

52. Interview with Claud Scott, October 27, 1961.

53. Mildred Harrington, "Village Store is Moore County," *Greensboro Daily News*, n.d. (in the files of John Maré).

54. Interview with Ben Owen, February 8, 1962. Steve Richardson had a pottery shop and hired potters to turn ware for him, but he was not a potter.

55. Interview with Claud Scott, October 27, 1961.

56. Interview with Ben Owen, February 8, 1962.

57. *Ibid.*

58. Agreement of lease between W. H. Scott and wife, Martha Jane Scott, and Jacques Busbee, June 15, 1922 (in the files of John Maré).

59. *Ibid.*

60. Deed Book 94, p. 16, Office of the Register of Deeds, Moore County, North Carolina, August 25, 1924, Carthage.

61. Deed Book 125, p. 416, Office of the Register of Deeds, Moore County, North Carolina, January 26, 1938, Carthage.

62. Interview with Claud Scott, October 27, 1961.

63. Burke Davis wrote that much of the furniture in the living room was said to have been made before 1800. "State Now Taking Note of Its Artistic Pottery . . . ," *Greensboro Daily News*, February 17, 1952.

64. The curtains were made from tobacco cloth which Mrs. Busbee dyed orange. (Handwritten notes by Clarence Thompson.)

65. At the time of the writer's visit, October 27, 1961.

66. [Juliana Busbee], "The Relation of Art to Life," MS, n.d. (in the files of Blackwell P. Robinson).

67. "Betty Graham Visits Jugtown," *News and Observer* (Raleigh), August 31, 1924.

68. "Ben Owen: Master Potter," folder in the shop of Ben Owen, Seagrove, N. C.

69. Interview with Ben Owen, December 11, 1961.

70. "To the Editor," p. 6.

71. Interview with Ben Owen, February 8, 1962.

72. Interviews with Ben Owen, October 7, 1961, and February 8, 1962.

73. Interview with Ben Owen, December 11, 1961.

74. Interview with Ben Owen, July 9, 1962.

75. Interview with Ben Owen, February 8, 1962.

76. "To the Editor," p. 7.

77. Letter from Thad Eure, Secretary of State, North Carolina, to writer, March 7, 1962, and letter from W. J. O'Brien, Assistant to the Director, Trademark Examining Operation, United States Patent Office, Washington, D. C., to writer, July 23, 1963.

78. Jacques Busbee, "A New Pottery for Connoisseurs: Jugtown Ware, A Descendant of Staffordshire," *California Arts and Architecture* (December, 1929), pp. 28-29.

79. Brochure, Person Hall Art Gallery, The University of North Carolina, Chapel Hill, N. C.

80. Interview with Ben Owen, February 8, 1962.

81. [Juliana Busbee], "Fashion Digest," MS, October, 1940, p. 9 (in the files of Blackwell P. Robinson).

82. Margaret O. Goldsmith, "Jugtown Pottery," *House Beautiful*, LII, No. 4 (October, 1922), 311.

83. Interview with Ben Owen, October 7, 1961.

84. Jane Hoagland, "New York Society of Craftsmen," *Art Center*, I, No. 9 (April, 1923), 28.

85. [Juliana Busbee], "B. & P. W. C.," p. 7.

86. Handwritten notes by Clarence Thompson (in the files of the writer).

87. Juliana R. Busbee, "Jugtown Comes of Age," *The State*, p. 7.

88. Elizabeth Smith, "Jugtown Pottery and Fans of Beautiful Design Put Out by Remarkable Store," *New York Telegram*, April —, 1923.

89. Program of the Zonta Club showing April, 1925, membership (in the files of John Maré).

90. Handwritten notes by Clarence Thompson (in the files of the writer).

91. Letter from the Office of the Chief Clerk, Shipping Department, to Jacques Busbee, n.d., Village Store stationery, New York (in the files of John Maré).

92. "On and Off the Avenue," *The New Yorker*, II, No. 6 (March 27, 1926), 40.

93. William A. McCall and Lelah Mae Crabbs, "Test Lesson 15," *Standard Test Lessons in Reading—Book 5* (Practice lessons for grades 5, 6, or 7) (New York: Bureau of Publications, Teachers College, Columbia University, 1926).

94. Interview with Ben Owen, February 8, 1962.

95. Clara Trenckmann, "Jugtown Potters Win Praise in Big N. Y. Exposition," syndicated article in *News and Observer* (Raleigh), May 31, 1925.

96. *Ibid.*

97. [Juliana Busbee], "B. & P. W. C." pp. 7-8.

98. Juliana Busbee, *The Bulletin of the American Ceramic Society*, p. 418. Mrs. Busbee maintained and sublet an apartment in New York at 57th Street and Park Avenue until several years before her death. (Interview with Clarence Thompson, July 17, 1962.)

99. Handwritten notes by Clarence Thompson.

100. Interview with John Maré, November 3, 1961.

101. Interview with Claud Scott, October 27, 1961.

102. Interview with Ben Owen, February 8, 1962.

103. Interview with Ben Owen, October 7, 1961.

104. Interview with William Bridges, August 31, 1962.

105. Interview with Woodrow W. Pruett, August 31, 1962.

106. Eleanor Mercein, "Adventurous Cookery," *Ladies Home Journal* (March, 1933), p. 105.

107. Letter from Mrs. Ernest L. Ives, Southern Pines, N. C., to writer, February 6, 1962.

108. Eleanor Mercein, *Ladies Home Journal*, p. 106.

109. Interview with Frank Manly, Preparator, North Carolina Museum of Art, July 25, 1962.

110. Bill Sharpe, "Pottery-Making Preserved as an Art by the Busbees," *Greensboro Daily News*, April 24, 1938.

111. Interview with Woodrow W. Pruett, August 31, 1962.

112. Eleanor Mercein, *Ladies Home Journal*, pp. 109-10.

113. Interview with Woodrow W. Pruett, August 31, 1962.

114. Interview with Clarence Thompson, July 24, 1962.

115. Interview with Woodrow W. Pruett, August 31, 1962.

116. *Ibid.*

117. *Ibid.*

118. *Ibid.*

119. Letter from Juliana Busbee to Woodrow Pruett, n.d. (in the files of Woodrow W. Pruett).

120. Letter from Juliana Busbee to Woodrow Pruett [July, 1956] (in the files of Woodrow W. Pruett).

121. Handwritten notes by Clarence Thompson.

122. Interview with Woodrow W. Pruett, August 31, 1962.

123. *Ibid.*

124. *Ibid.*

125. Handwritten notes by Clarence Thompson.

126. Interview with Wade Owen, August 21, 1962.

127. Interview with Woodrow W. Pruett, August 31, 1962.

128. *Ibid.*

129. Interview with William Bridges, August 31, 1962.

130. Interview with Woodrow W. Pruett, August 31, 1962.

131. Letter from Mrs. Ernest L. Ives to writer, February 6, 1962.

132. Letter from Burke Davis, Williamsburg, Virginia, to writer, October 31, 1961.

133. Interview with Woodrow W. Pruett, August 31, 1962.

134. *Ibid.*

135. Letter from Juliana Busbee to Woodrow W. Pruett, signed "Cinderella of the ashes," n.d. (in the files of Woodrow W. Pruett).

136. Isabelle Bowen Henderson, letter of recommendation when Juliana Busbee was being considered for an honorary degree at The Woman's College of the University of North Carolina, n.d. (in the files of Blackwell P. Robinson). (Verifax copy.)

137. Juliana Busbee, *The E. S. C. Quarterly*, p. 61.

138. Ivan Stowe Clark, *The Journal of Geography*, p. 224.

139. *Ibid.*, p. 225.

140. Ben Dixon MacNeill, *News and Observer* (Raleigh), April 3, 1927.

141. A. T. Robertson, Jr., "Meet the Busbees, of Jugtown," *The State*, I, No. 25 (November 18, 1933), 16.

142. Juliana Busbee, *The E. S. C. Quarterly*, p. 61.

143. "Jugs From Carolina Hills," *The Christian Science Monitor*, May 18, 1938.

144. Letter from Juliana Busbee to Woodrow Pruett, n.d. (in the files of Woodrow W. Pruett).

145. Juliana R. Busbee, "Jugtown Comes of Age," *The State*, p. 7.

146. Brochure, Person Hall Art Gallery, The University of North Carolina, Chapel Hill.

NOTES TO CHAPTER III

1. Letter from W. Kerr Scott, Governor of North Carolina, to Mrs. Jacques Busbee, November 4, 1949 (in the files of John Maré).

2. Jane Hall, "Winners Named by Art Society," *News and Observer* (Raleigh), December 1, 1949.

3. "Jugtown. Jacques Busbee, 1875-1947," folder accompanying the exhibit (in the files of the North Carolina Museum of Art, Raleigh, N. C.).

4. *Ibid.*

5. "The Jacques Busbee Memorial Collection of Jugtown Pottery," guide sheet (in the files of the North Carolina Museum of Art).

6. Lucy Cherry Crisp, press release, n.d. (in the files of the North Carolina Museum of Art). (Mimeographed.)

7. Interview with Ben F. Williams, January 25, 1962.

8. Letter from Mrs. M. W. Crocker, Columbus, Ohio, to writer, February 15, 1963 (in the files of the writer).

9. Juliana Busbee, *The Bulletin of the American Ceramic Society*, p. 418.

10. Earl Dean, "Artistry, Not Profit, Motivates the Potter," *News and Observer* (Raleigh), October 24, 1948.

11. Fourteen affidavits and three notarized letters from friends of Juliana Busbee, noting changes in her mind and memory (in the files of Herbert F. Seawell, Jr., Carthage, N. C.).

12. Interview with Ben Owen, December 11, 1961.

13. "Negotiations Regarding the Future of

Jugtown," n.n., n.d., p. 1 (in the files of Blackwell P. Robinson). (Mimeographed.)

14. *Ibid.*, p. 1.

15. Mrs. W. A. Mahler, Administrative Assistant for the State Literary and Historical Association; Mrs. Joye Jordan of the Hall of History; Ben Williams, Curator, North Carolina Museum of Art; James B. Byrnes, Acting Director, North Carolina Museum of Art. (*Ibid.*, p. 2.)

16. Letter from Christopher Crittenden to Mrs. Jacques Busbee (with changes made by Ben Williams and James B. Byrnes), June 9, 1958 (in the files of the Department of Archives and History, Raleigh, N. C.).

17. "Negotiations Regarding the Future of Jugtown," p. 2.

18. *Ibid.*, p. 3.

19. Letter from Christopher Crittenden, Director of the North Carolina Department of Archives and History, to writer, September 6, 1962.

20. [Isabelle Bowen Henderson], MS on circumstances leading to the establishment of Jugtown, Incorporated [April 27, 1959], p. 1 (in the files of the Department of Archives and History, Raleigh, N. C.). (Mimeographed.) Interview with Ottway Burton, August 21, 1962; letter from Mr. Burton to writer, January 21, 1963.

21. Interview with Blackwell P. Robinson, February 26, 1962. Meetings were held at Jugtown, in Mr. Burton's office in Asheboro, and in Herbert F. Seawell's office in Carthage. At one or all meetings were Mrs. Isabelle Henderson, Mr. and Mrs. Burke Davis, Mr. and Mrs. Ben Williams, Phillips Russell, and Dr. and Mrs. Blackwell P. Robinson.

22. *Ibid.*

23. "Articles of Incorporation of Jugtown, Incorporated," 86676, filed with the Secretary of State, March 12, 1959, Raleigh.

24. *Ibid.*

25. Warranty Deed, "Mrs. Juliana Busbee et al to Jugtown, Inc.," December 5, 1958, acknowledged before a Notary Public in Wake County, North Carolina, but unrecorded (in the files of Herbert F. Seawell, Jr.).

26. Interview with Blackwell P. Robinson, February 26, 1962.

27. [Henderson], MS on circumstances . . . , p. 2.

28. Later withdrew.

29. "Memo to Members of Jugtown, Inc.," December 15, 1958 (in the files of Blackwell P. Robinson).

30. Letter from Zebulon Judd to Ben F. Williams, n.d. [received shortly before February 6, 1959] (in the files of Blackwell P. Robinson). (Verifax copy.)

31. [Henderson] MS on circumstances . . . , p. 2.

32. *Ibid.*; after Mrs. Judd's death, the deed was returned by Dr. Judd's lawyer, stating, "He [Dr. Judd] does not think he has any interest in the property itself." (Letter from Knox M. McMillan to Mrs. Isabelle B. Henderson, May 6, 1959 [in the files of Herbert F. Seawell, Jr.].)

33. Interview with Ben Owen, November 22, 1961.

34. "A Sandhill Citizen—John Maré," *Sandhill Citizen*, May 11, 1961.

35. Letter from Oliver R. Grace, partner of Sterling, Grace & Co., to writer, January 21, 1964.

36. "A Sandhill Citizen—John Maré," *Sandhill Citizen*, May 11, 1961.

37. Interview with John Maré, November 3, 1961.

38. Agreement between Juliana Busbee and John Maré, March 2, 1959 (in the files of P. H. Wilson, Carthage, N. C.). (Carbon copy.)

39. The memorial—the cabin at Jugtown that was to become a museum—was to be a personal project of John Maré; the State was not involved. Before his death, Mr. Maré had begun to assemble mementos on Jugtown from people who knew the Busbees, and he was also collecting information on the Jugtown story. Some changes were being made in the furnishings. A date for the anticipated opening had not been set. (Telephone conversation with John Maré, March 26, 1962.)

40. Agreement between Juliana Busbee and John Maré.

41. "Articles of Incorporation of Jacques and Juliana Busbee's Jugtown, Inc.," 86605, Book 6, p. 368, Office of the Clerk of Court, Moore County, North Carolina, March 11, 1959, Carthage.

42. Warranty Deed, "Juliana Busbee to Jacques and Juliana Busbee's Jugtown, Inc.," Deed Book 228, p. 521, Office of the Register of Deeds, Moore County, North Carolina, March 11, 1959, Carthage.

43. [Henderson], MS on circumstances . . . , p. 2.

44. Letter from Thad Eure, Secretary of State, North Carolina, to writer, March 7, 1962.

45. Letter from Mrs. William A. Mahler, Jr., to John Maré, March 23, 1959 (in the files of John Maré).

46. Letter from John Maré to Mrs. William A. Mahler, Jr., n.d. (in the files of John Maré).

47. Interview with Ben Owen, October 27, 1961.

48. Interview with Mrs. Ben Owen, October 7, 1961.

49. [Henderson], MS on circumstances . . . , p. 2.

50. Letter from C. Malcolm Watkins, Curator, Division of Cultural History, Smithsonian Institu-tion, United States National Museum, Washing-ton, D. C., to writer, October 24, 1961.

51. Interview with Wade Owen, son of Ben Owen, August 21, 1962.

52. *Jugtown, Incorporated* v. *John Maré and The Jacques and Juliana Busbee's Jugtown, Incor-porated*, "Complaint," 6800, Office of the Clerk of Court, Moore County, North Carolina, April 22, 1959, Carthage.

53. *Ibid.*, "Temporary Restraining Order and Appointment of Trustee."

54. Jane Hall, *News and Observer* (Raleigh), May 10, 1959.

55. Fourteen affidavits and three notarized let-ters from friends of Juliana Busbee; letters from A. A. Vanore, M.D., "To Whom It May Con-cern," April 30, 1959, and C. R. Monroe, M.D., "To Whom It May Concern," April 30, 1959 (in the files of Herbert F. Seawell, Jr.).

56. Carbon copy of a letter from Henderson, Williams, and Robinson.

57. *Jugtown, Inc., & Mrs. Louise R. Jordan, next friend of Mrs. Juliana Busbee* v. *John Maré and The Jacques and Juliana Busbee's Jugtown, Inc.*, "Petition for Appointment of Next Friend in this Action," 6826, Office of the Clerk of Court, Moore County, North Carolina, May 12, 1959, Carthage.

58. *Ibid.*, "Order."

59. Carbon copy of a letter from Gordon W. Blackwell, Chancellor, The Woman's College of the University of North Carolina, Greensboro, N. C., to Mrs. Juliana Royster Busbee, May 13, 1959 (in the files of Blackwell P. Robinson).

60. "Citation for Mrs. Busbee," MS read by Blackwell P. Robinson at the Commencement Exercises (in the files of Blackwell P. Robinson).

61. [Juliana Busbee], "For Lawrence of Lum-berton."

62. Interview with Claud Scott, October 27, 1961.

63. *Mrs. Louise R. Jordan, Next Friend of Juliana Busbee and Jugtown, Inc., v. John Maré and Jack and Juliana Busbee's Jugtown, Inc.,* "Restraining Order, Complaint, and Bond," 6826, Office of the Clerk of Court, Moore County, North Carolina, June 2, 1959, Carthage.

64. *Jugtown v. Maré,* "Judgment of Non-Suit," 6800, Office of the Clerk of Court, Moore County, North Carolina, June 2, 1959, Carthage.

65. *Jordan v. Maré,* "Petition and Motion of Mrs. Juliana Busbee," 6826, Office of the Clerk of Court, Moore County, North Carolina, June 13, 1959, Carthage.

66. Letter from Isabelle Bowen Henderson to "Dear Friends of Jugtown," October 8, 1959 (in the files of Blackwell P. Robinson). (Mimeographed.)

67. *In the matter of Juliana Busbee,* "Verdict," 7727, Office of the Clerk of Court, Moore County, North Carolina, July 30, 1959, Carthage.

68. *In the matter of Juliana Busbee,* "Order," 7727, Office of the Clerk of Court, Moore County, North Carolina, August 5, 1959, Carthage.

69. *Jordan v. Maré,* "Consent Order," 6826, Office of the Clerk of Court, Moore County, North Carolina, August 10, 1959, Carthage.

70. *Jordan v. Maré,* "Motion of Defendant to Dissolve Temporary Restraining Order," 5505, Office of the Clerk of Court, Moore County, North Carolina, November 16, 1959, Carthage.

71. *Jordan v. Maré,* "Judgment," 24112, Office of the Clerk of Court, Moore County, North Carolina, December 8, 1959, Carthage.

72. "Jugtown Cleared of Legal Action," *Greensboro Daily News,* December 9, 1959.

73. "Jugtown Litigation is Brought to End," *Greenboro Daily News,* March 5, 1960.

74. Interview with John Maré, November 4, 1961.

75. *Ibid.*

76. "Juliana Busbee of Jugtown," *Greensboro Daily News,* with a quotation from Valerie Nicholson, March 6, 1962. Both Mr. and Mrs. Busbee were cremated and their ashes were scattered at Jugtown. Mr. Maré began the scattering of Juliana Busbee's ashes on the day of the services for her and the scattering was completed on the day of the services for Mr. Maré. (Interview with Howard C. Broughton, Lawyer, August 21, 1962, and letter from Mr. Broughton to writer, February 14, 1963).

77. Interview with Howard C. Broughton, attorney for John Maré, August 21, 1962.

78. "A Sandhill Citizen—John Maré," *Sandhill Citizen,* May 11, 1961.

79. "Last Will and Testament of John Maré," 8369, Book V, p. 511, Office of the Clerk of Court, Moore County, North Carolina, June 14, 1962, Carthage.

80. *Ibid.* The Executors were authorized to "hire and discharge officers and employees, fix their compensation and define their duties; and similarly to employ, compensate, and discharge agents, attorneys, consultants, accountants and such other representatives as my Executors may deem appropriate."

NOTES TO CHAPTER IV

1. Jacques Busbee, "To the Editor," pp. 6-7.

2. Joe Q. Mitchell, "Busbees Exhibit Art of Jugtown to Playmakers," *Chapel Hill Weekly,* February 17, 1928.

3. Letter from Mrs. Albert Lathrop, Asheville, N. C., to writer, March 3, 1962. Mrs. Lathrop wrote that Mr. Busbee mentioned often to her that certain pieces were to go to the Metropolitan Museum.

4. Mildred Harrington, "The Busbees and Jugtown, Laugh is on Tar Heelia," *Greensboro Daily News*, December 9, 1923.

5. Letter from Mrs. May Davis Hill, Art Librarian, The Ackland Art Center, to writer, January 31, 1962.

6. Letter from Mrs. Sue O. Armstrong, Keeper of Collections, The Charleston Museum, to writer, December 27, 1961.

7. Letter from Henry Hawley, Assistant Curator of Decorative Arts, The Cleveland Museum of Art (with information supplied by Doris E. Dunlavy, Head of the Extension Exhibition Department, Cleveland Museum of Art), to writer, December 8, 1961.

8. Letter from Mrs. Marjorie Jackson, Director, The Greenville Art Center, to writer, February 14, 1962.

9. "The Jacques Busbee Memorial Collection . . . ," guide sheet.

10. Letter from C. Malcolm Watkins, Curator, Division of Cultural History, Smithsonian Institution, to writer, October 24, 1961.

11. Jacques Busbee, *California Arts and Architecture*, pp. 28-29.

12. Juliana Busbee, "Jugtown Pottery," *Fashion Digest* (Winter, 1941), p. 72.

13. Order book of Jugtown Pottery for 1950 (in the files of John Maré).

14. Interview with Russell Thompson, April 5, 1962.

15. Clara Trenckmann, *News and Observer* (Raleigh), May 31, 1925; "Southerners Open Their Exposition: Industrial Story of 14 States is Told by Colorful Displays at Grand Central Palace," *New York Times*, May 12, 1925, p. 11.

16. Playbill for *Sun Up*, Princess Theatre, Broadway, New York, n.d. (in the files of John Maré).

17. Joe Q. Mitchell, *Chapel Hill Weekly*, February 17, 1928.

18. Newspaper clipping, n.n., n.d. (in the files of John Maré).

19. Newspaper clipping, n.n., n.d. (in the files of John Maré).

20. Calendar for 1930, Dixie Chapter, United Daughters of the Confederacy, Columbus, Ohio (in the files of John Maré).

21. "Lee Plaza Hotel Guide," Detroit, Mich., August, 1930, p. 6 (in the files of John Maré).

22. "Caroline Kimball Speaks on Jugtown Pottery," *Carmel-by-Sea*, n.d., September, 1930 (in the files of John Maré).

23. *Progressive in Spirit and Published in the Interest of Pawhuska and Osage County*, Pawhuska, Okla., January 30, 1931 (in the files of John Maré).

24. "Mrs. Busbee is heard by U. N. C. Summer Pupils," newspaper clipping, n.n., July 15, 1931 (in the files of John Maré).

25. Clipping from *News and Observer* (Raleigh), April 15, 1934 (in the files of John Maré).

26. Jean Eliot, "Jugtown Pottery Put on Exhibit in Binyon Garden," *Washington Herald*, May 16, 1935.

27. Letter from Mrs. Juanita MacDougald Melchoir, a past Director of Art in the schools of North Carolina, now in Syracuse, N. Y., to writer, March 16, 1962.

28. Letter from Allen H. Eaton to writer, December 1, 1961. The Southern Highland Handicraft Guild co-operated with the Department of Agriculture in the preparation of an exhibition of rural arts held in Washington, D. C., in November, 1937, in connection with the Seventy-fifth Anniversary celebration of the Department; Allen H. Eaton, *Handicrafts of the Southern Highlands With an Account of the Rural Handicraft Movement in the United States and Suggestions for the*

Wider Use of Handicrafts in Adult Education and Recreation (New York: Russell Sage Foundation, 1937), p. 252.

29. Marion Wright, "Arts and Artists," *Charlotte Observer*, January 7, 1940.

30. "Howard University Gallery of Arts," program folder (in the files of Blackwell P. Robinson).

31. Letter from Romaine Stec, Curator of Decorative Arts, The Baltimore Museum of Art, to writer, October 30, 1961, citing *Contemporary American Crafts*, Exhibition Catalogue by The Baltimore Museum of Art, February 11 to March 19, 1944, Baltimore, Md., p. 19.

32. Conversation with Mrs. David D. Jones, wife of the late President of Bennett College, March 12, 1962.

33. Mamie H. Braddy, *Twin City Sentinel* (Winston-Salem), December 13, 1947, p. 10.

34. Jane Hall, "Art Society Meets Today, Opening Annual Series Here," *News and Observer* (Raleigh), November 30, 1949.

35. Lucy Cherry Crisp, "For Immediate Release," n.d. (in the files of the North Carolina Museum of Art). (Mimeographed.)

36. "The Jacques Busbee Memorial Collection . . . ," guide sheet.

37. Letter, Lucy Cherry Crisp to Mrs. J. D. Whitfield, January 22, 1951 (in the files of the North Carolina Museum of Art).

38. Letters from William B. O'Neal, Curator, University of Virginia, n.d. (in the files of the North Carolina Museum of Art).

39. "Exhibit of Jugtown Pottery Featured at Catawba Library," *Evening Post* (Salisbury), May 28, 1954.

40. Letter from Sara Little, Decoration Editor, *House Beautiful*, to Mrs. Busbee, February 28, 1955 (in the files of John Maré); letter from Roy F. Williams, Director, Office of International Trade Fairs, Department of Commerce, Washington, D. C., to Mrs. Busbee, August 1, 1955 (in the files of John Maré); newspaper clipping, n.n., n.d. (in the files of Mrs. Ben Owen, confirmed by Mrs. Owen in an interview, December 11, 1961).

41. "Jugtown Ware Goes on Exhibit," *News and Observer* (Raleigh), April 26, 1959.

42. Letter from Mrs. Albert H. Lathrop to writer, March 3, 1962.

43. Interview with Mrs. Mary John Resch, Raleigh, N. C., March 22, 1962.

44. "Jugtown Featured on Radio Program," *Sandhill Citizen* (Aberdeen), November 30, 1961.

45. "Twin City Datebook," *Journal and Sentinel* (Winston-Salem), April 1, 1962.

46. Elene Foster, *New York Tribune*, July 27, 1919.

47. Amy Richards Colton and Arthur W. Colton, "Pottery That Plays A Part in Garden and Loggia," *The Garden Magazine*, XXXVII, No. 5 (July, 1923), 317.

48. Mildred Harrington, *Greensboro Daily News*, December 9, 1923.

49. "Betty Graham Visits Jugtown," *News and Observer* (Raleigh), August 31, 1924.

50. "Jugtown," *Pinehurst Outlook*, February 28, 1931.

51. Eaton, *Handicrafts of the Southern Highlands*, p. 211.

52. "Sandhill Potters Use Old Method, Turning Out Beautiful Pieces by Hand," *Philadelphia Inquirer*, April 24, 1938.

53. Gertrude Carraway, "Jugtown Survives as Center of Important Pottery Craft," *News and Observer* (Raleigh), December 15, 1940.

54. Dorothy Liebes, Thomas Aitken, Jr., and Gertrude S. Carraway (told by them), "What's

Happening in USA?" *The American Home,* XXVI, No. 1 (June, 1941), 62-63.

55. Dorothy Noyce, "The Pottery of Jugtown," *Ford Times,* CI, No. 3 (March, 1959), 25-26.

56. Gertrude Carraway, "Jugtown Survives . . . ," *News and Observer,* (Raleigh), December 15, 1940.

57. Letter from John Coolidge, Farmington, Conn., to writer, March 26, 1962.. He added, "At one time my mother and some friends had a place in the mountains in North Carolina and perhaps they bought the pottery to use there. This place was disposed of before my mother's death and perhaps the pottery was also sold or went to one of the other owners of the property."

58. Forrest Lockey of Aberdeen, N. C., wrote, "He [John F. Kennedy] expressed a great deal of pleasure to get something from Jugtown and left the meeting with one under each arm to take to his home." Letter from Forrest Lockey to Mrs. Valerie Nicholson, Southern Pines, n.d. (in the files of John Maré).

59. "Kennedy Pleased by Gift from Jugtown," *Fayetteville Observer,* December 18, 1960.

60. Mavis Perry, "Jugtown Ware," *News and Courier* (Charleston, S. C.), February 18, 1962.

61. Letter from Allen H. Eaton to writer, December 1, 1961.

62. Included in a letter from Henry Hawley to writer, December 8, 1961.

63. Letter from Ben F. Williams (unsigned) "To Whom It May Concern," recommending Juliana Busbee for an honorary degree, n.d. (in the files of Blackwell P. Robinson). (Photostat.)

64. M. C. Richards, "Leach: East and West," *Craft Horizons,* XX, No. 4 (July/August, 1960), 38. Quoting Bernard Leach at a talk at the Donnell Public Library in New York City on May 24, 1960.

65. Letter from Bernard Leach, The Pottery, St. Ives, Cornwall, England, to writer, March 24, 1962.

66. Letter from C. Malcolm Watkins to writer, October 24, 1961.

NOTES TO CHAPTER V

1. Henrich Ries, "Clay Deposits and Clay Industry in North Carolina," Bulletin 13, *North Carolina Geological Survey,* 1897.

2. W. S. Bayley, "The Kaolins of North Carolina," Bulletin 29, *North Carolina Geological and Economic Survey,* 1925.

3. Sam D. Broadhurst, "White Residual Clays of the Volcanic Slate Belt in North Carolina," Information Circular 8, Division of Mineral Resources, North Carolina Department of Conservation and Development, p. 4.

4. *Ibid.,* pp. 6-7.

5. *Ibid.,* p. 18.

6. *Ibid.,* p. 19.

7. Interview with Ben Owen, October 18, 1961.

8. Two types of ware were made at Jugtown— earthenware and stoneware. Daniel Rhodes, in his book *Clay and Glazes for the Potter* (New York: Greenberg, 1957), notes the differences in the earthenware clays and the stoneware clays: "Stoneware clays are plastic clays which mature or become vitreous at 1200° to 1300°. Their fired color ranges from a very light grey or buff to a darker grey or brown. Stoneware clays are secondary, or sedimentary, clays" (p. 19). "Most of the usable clay found in nature might be called 'earthenware' clay or common clay. These clays contain iron and other mineral impurities in sufficient quantity to cause the clay to become tight and hard-fired at about 950° to 1100°. In the raw, such a clay is red, brown, greenish, or grey, as a result of the presence of iron oxide" (p. 20).

9. Letters from Stephen G. Conrad, Assistant State Geologist, Division of Mineral Resources, Department of Conservation and Development, Raleigh, N. C., to writer, January 25, 1962, and October 15, 1962.

NOTES TO CHAPTER VI

1. Jacques Busbee, "To the Editor," p. 9.

2. Jacques Busbee, *California Arts and Architecture*, pp. 28-29.

3. Interview with Ben Owen, December 11, 1961.

4. Russell Thompson has these pieces in his collection.

5. [Juliana Busbee], "Fashion Digest," p. 9.

6. No record has been kept of the number and type of different shapes made at Jugtown. Mr. Maré attempted to get examples of the original shapes produced. Some hand-molded pieces in animal shapes were made again, as well as some Chinese-inspired figurines. Three new shapes of bowls were introduced into the Jugtown line. (Interview with John Maré, November 4, 1961.)

7. [Jacques Busbee], "A Colonial Hangover," p. 4.

8. [Juliana Busbee], "Fashion Digest," p. 9.

9. Letter from C. Malcolm Watkins to writer, October 24, 1961.

10. Jacques Busbee, "To the Editor," p. 8.

11. Interview with Ben Owen, November 22, 1961.

12. *Ibid*.

NOTES TO CHAPTER VII

1. Interview with Ben Owen, March 17, 1962.

2. Margaret O. Goldsmith, *House Beautiful*, p. 311.

3. Letter from Ben Owen to writer [April 2, 1962].

4. Under the management of John Maré, two new glazes were added to the eight original glazes made at Jugtown: "Black Ankle," which is a mixture of the "Frogskin" and the white; and "Accidental," which is an orange-brown tinged with green. (Interview with Mr. Maré, November 4, 1961.)

5. Value refers to lightness and darkness.

6. Slip, according to Russell Thompson, a student of ceramics, "is made from clay which is made into a creamy consistency." (Interview with Russell Thompson, April 5, 1962.) The slip used on the orange ware is made from blue or gray stoneware clay. (Letter from Ben Owen to writer, April 2, 1962.)

7. Letter from Ben Owen to writer, April 2, 1962.

8. *Ibid*. "Varied by mixture of clay. Medium is made of 2 to 3 kinds of clay which is necessary to get the proper working consistency."

9. Interview with Russell Thompson, April 5, 1962.

10. Interview with Ben Owen, February 8, 1962.

11. Interview with Ben Williams, March 22, 1962.

12. Interview with Ben Owen, February 8, 1962.

13. Clarence Thompson says that Mr. Busbee told him the secret ingredient for the blue-green. (Handwritten notes by Clarence Thompson.)

14. Interview with Blackwell P. Robinson, April 16, 1962.

15. Interview with John Maré, November 4, 1961.

16. The blue-green was of high value, weak intensity, without red spots. Three pieces were

made in the blue-green. (Interview with Vernon Owens and Bobby Owens, August 25, 1962.)

17. Interview with Ben Owen, February 8, 1962.

NOTES TO CHAPTER VIII

1. Juliana R. Busbee, *The State*, p. 22.

2. Interview with Ben Owen, October 7, 1961.

3. Mr. Hajime Kato, a well-known pottery artist in Japan, visited Jugtown in 1957, and, following his visit, a reporter wrote that among Jugtown's features that reminded Kato of the Orient was the clay-grinding mill powered by a mule. (Caroline Ingraham, "Hajime Kato: Potter of Yokohama," reprint from *Far Eastern Ceramic Bulletin*, IX, Nos. 1-2 [March-June, 1957], n.p. [in the files of the North Carolina Museum of Art].) Mr. Kato turned a piece of ware on the wheel at Jugtown, and the piece is now in the North Carolina Museum of Art. (Interview with Ben Williams, October 2, 1961.)

4. Interview with Ben Owen, November 22, 1961.

5. "Negotiations Regarding the Future of Jugtown," p. 3.

6. A power-driven hammer mill was later used to grind the clay to a powder; then it was transferred to the pug mill for mixing. (Interview with John Maré, November 3, 1961.)

7. Interview with Ben Owen, October 18, 1961.

8. Interview with Ben Owen, December 11, 1961.

9. Interviews with and demonstrations by Ben Owen, October 7, November 22, December 11, 1961; February 8, March 17, 1962.

10. Interview with Ben Owen, March 17, 1962.

11. Personal observation, October 27, 1961.

12. [Jacques Busbee], "A Colonial Hangover," p. 5.

13. Interview with John Maré, November 4, 1961.

14. Interview with Ben Owen, February 8, 1962.

15. *Ibid.*

16. Interview with Boyce Yow, November 22, 1961. Blasting on the earthenware kiln was for a shorter period of time.

17. Interview with Ben Owen, October 7, 1961.

18. *Ibid.*

19. Interview with Ben Owen, October 18, 1961.

20. Interview with Russell Thompson, October 4, 1961.

21. Interview with Mrs. Ben Owen, October 7, 1961.

22. Juliana Busbee, MS on Jugtown history, n.d. (in the files of Blackwell P. Robinson).

NOTES TO CHAPTER IX

1. One visitor reported, "In those early days at Jugtown invitations were issued 'M.P.'—mud permitting. A visit with the Busbees in their cozy log house was well worth braving the mire." (Bonnie Angelo Levy, "Jugtown's Mrs. Busbee Vital to State's Crafts," *Twin City Sentinel* [Winston-Salem], March 29, 1951.)

2. "Can Jugtown Go On," editorial in the *Winston-Salem Journal*, August 28, 1962.

3. Beverly Wolter, "State's Pottery Art Faces a Crucial Era; Lack of Skilled Craftsmen Hits Home," *Journal and Sentinel* (Winston-Salem), September 1, 1963.

Books

Arnett, Ethel Stephens. *Greensboro, North Carolina: The County Seat of Guilford.* Written under the direction of Walter Clinton Jackson. Chapel Hill: The University of North Carolina Press, 1955.

Eaton, Allen H. *Handicrafts of the Southern Highlands With an Account of the Rural Handicraft Movement in the United States and Suggestions for the Wider Use of Handicrafts in Adult Education and Recreation.* New York: Russell Sage Foundation, 1937.

Fries, Adelaide L. (ed.). *Records of the Moravians in North Carolina.* Vol. I. 1752-1771. Raleigh: Edwards and Broughton Printing Company, State Printers, 1922.

Lefler, Hugh T. *History of North Carolina.* Vol. II. New York: Lewis Historical Publishing Co., Inc., 1956.

Lefler, Hugh Talmage, and Newsome, Albert Ray. *North Carolina: The History of a Southern State.* Chapel Hill: The University of North Carolina Press, 1954.

Marquis, Albert Nelson (ed.). *Who's Who in America: A Biographical Dictionary of Notable Living Men and Women of the United States.* Vol. XIII. Chicago: A. N. Marquis & Company, 1924-1925.

Ramsay, John. *American Potters and Pottery.* Clinton, Mass.: Hale, Cushman, & Flint, Colonial Press, Inc., 1939.

Rhodes, Daniel. *Clay and Glazes for the Potter.* New York: Greenberg, 1957.

Rice, A. H., and Stoudt, John Baer. *The Shenandoah Pottery.* Strasburg, Virginia: Shenandoah Publishing House, Inc., 1929.

Robinson, Blackwell P. *A History of Moore County, North Carolina. 1747-1847.* Southern Pines, N. C.: Moore County Historical Association, 1956.

Webster's Seventh New Collegiate Dictionary. Springfield: G. & C. Merriam Co., 1963.

Periodicals and Newspapers

"A Sandhill Citizen—John Maré," *Sandhill Citizen* (Aberdeen), May 11, 1961.

Bayley, W. S. "The Kaolins of North Carolina," *North Carolina Geological and Economic Survey*, Bulletin 29, 1925.

"Ben Owen: Master Potter," folder in the shop of Ben Owen, Seagrove, N. C.

"Betty Graham Visits Jugtown," *News and Observer* (Raleigh), August 31, 1924.

Braddy, Mamie H. "University Honors Busbee as Master of Pottery Art," *Twin City Sentinel* (Winston-Salem), December 13, 1947, p. 10.

Broadhurst, Sam D. "White Residual Clays of the Volcanic Slate Belt in North Carolina," Information Circular 8, North Carolina Department of Conservation and Development, Division of Mineral Resources, 1950.

Busbee, Jacques. "A New Pottery for Connoisseurs: Jugtown Ware, A Descendant of Staffordshire," *California Arts and Architecture* (December, 1929), pp. 28-29.

_____. "Jugtown Pottery," *Ceramic Age* (October, 1929), pp. 127-30.

_____. "My Great Aunt and 'Carolina,'" *The North Carolina Booklet*, XII, No. 4 The North Carolina Society, Daughters of the Revolution, October, 1911), 99-104.

_____. "Kill Devil Hill," *The North Carolina Booklet*, XI, No. 2 (Raleigh, N. C.: (Raleigh, N. C.: The North Carolina Society, Daughters of the Revolution, April, 1913), 211-15.

Busbee, Mrs. Jacques. "Pottery in N. C.," Letter to the Editor, *News and Observer* (Raleigh), July 21, 1929.

Busbee, Juliana. "Jugtown Pottery: A New Way for Old Jugs," *The Bulletin of the American Ceramic Society*, XVI, No. 10 (October, 1937), 415, 418-19.

_____. "Jugtown Pottery," *Fashion Digest* (Winter, 1941), p. 72.

_____. "New Ways for Old Jugs—Art in Jugtown Pottery," *The E. S. C. Quarterly*, V, No. 2-3 (Spring-Summer, 1947), 60-61.

Busbee, Juliana R. "Age-Old Profession Now Flourishes in Sand Hills," *News and Observer* (Raleigh), June 5, 1927.

_____. "Jugtown Comes of Age," *The State*, V, No. 3 (June 19, 1937), 6-7, 22.

"Busbee Home Will Go Soon," *News and Observer* (Raleigh), October 12, 1914.

"Can Jugtown Go On?" *Winston-Salem Journal*, August 28, 1962.

Carraway, Gertrude. "Jugtown Survives as Center of Important Pottery Craft," *News and Observer* (Raleigh), December 15, 1940.

Clark, Ivan Stowe. "An Isolated Industry: Pottery of North Carolina," *The Journal of Geography*, XXV, No. 6 (September, 1926), 222-28.

Colton, Amy Richards, and Colton, Arthur W. "Pottery That Plays A Part in Garden and Loggia," *The Garden Magazine*, XXXVII, No. 5 (July, 1923), 317.

Daniels, Jonathan. "Tarheel Capital," *Holiday*, XIX, No. 2 (February, 1956), 40-41.

Davis, Burke. "State Now Taking Note of Its Artistic Pottery; Chinese and Native Designs; Jugtown Reclaims an Old Art," *Greensboro Daily News*, February 17, 1952.

Dean, Earl. "Artistry, Not Profit, Motivates the Potter," *News and Observer* (Raleigh), October 24, 1948.

Dunnagan, M. R. "Pottery Making, Ancient Art, Increasing in State," *The E. S. C. Quarterly*, V, No. 2-3 (Spring-Summer, 1947), 53-55.

Eliot, Jean. "Jugtown Pottery Put on Exhibit in Binyon Garden," *Washington Herald*, May 16, 1935.

"Exhibit of Jugtown Pottery Featured at Catawba Library," *Evening Post* (Salisbury), May 28, 1954.

"Five Remarkable Women Who are Winning Fame as Business Leaders," *Evening Telegram* (New York), May 27, 1923.

Foster, Elene. "A One Hundred Per Cent American Shop," *New York Tribune*, July 27, 1919.

Garrett, Garet. "Points South," *The Saturday Evening Post*, CCIII, No. 5 (August 2, 1930), 6-7, 9.

Goldsmith, Margaret O. "Jugtown Pottery," *House Beautiful*, LII, No. 4 (October, 1922), 311.

Greaves-Walker, A. F. "Demand for Art Pottery Spurs Revival of Craft in Carolina," *News and Observer* (Raleigh), July 7, 1929.

Hall, Jane. "Art Society Meets Today, Opening Annual Series Here," *News and Observer* (Raleigh), November 30, 1949.

_____. "Judge Vacates Restraining Order Regarding Famed Pottery Center," *News and Observer* (Raleigh), May 10, 1959.

_____. "Winners Named by Art Society," *News and Observer* (Raleigh), December 1, 1949.

Harrington, Mildred. "Interesting People: The Master Potter of Jugtown," *The American Magazine*, CIII, No. 6 (June, 1927), 72-74.

_____. "The Busbees and Jugtown, Laugh is on Tar Heelia," *Greensboro Daily News*, December 9, 1923.

Hoagland, Jane. "New York Society of Craftsmen," *Art Center*, I, No. 9 (April, 1923), 28.

Ingraham, Caroline. "Hajime Kato: Potter of Yokohama," reprint from *Far Eastern Ceramic Bulletin*, IX, Nos. 1-2 (March-June, 1957), n.p. (in the files of the North Carolina Museum of Art).

"Johnson Jug Factory: Catawba County Boasts Original 'Jugtown' Site," *Hickory Daily Record*, U. D. C. Edition, February, 1938.

"Jugs From Carolina Hills," *The Christian Science Monitor*, May 18, 1938.

"Jugtown," *Pinehurst Outlook*, February 28, 1931.

"Jugtown Cleared of Legal Action," *Greensboro Daily News*, December 9, 1959.

"Jugtown Featured on Radio Program," *Sandhill Citizen* (Aberdeen), November 30, 1961.

"Jugtown Litigation is Brought to End," *Greensboro Daily News*, March 5, 1960.

"Jugtown Ware Goes on Exhibit," *News and Observer* (Raleigh), April 26, 1959.

"Juliana Busbee of Jugtown," *Greenboro Daily News*, March 6, 1962.

"Kennedy Pleased by Gift from Jugtown," *Fayetteville Observer*, December 18, 1960.

Lawrence, R. C. "The Story [of] Jacques Busbee, Poet of Pottery, and of Our Own Jugtown," *Pilot* (Southern Pines and Aberdeen), December 15, 1939.

Levy, Bonnie Angelo. "Jugtown's Mrs. Busbee Vital to State's Crafts," *Twin City Sentinel* (Winston-Salem), March 29, 1951.

Liebes, Dorothy, Aitken, Thomas, Jr., and Carraway, Gertrude S. "What's Happening in USA?" *The American Home*, XXVI, No. 1 (June, 1941), 62-63.

McCall, William A., and Crabbs, Lelah Mae. "Test Lesson 15," *Standard Test Lessons in Reading—Book 5* (Practice Lessons for grades 5, 6, or 7) (New York: Bureau of Publications, Teachers College, Columbia University, 1926).

MacNeill, Ben Dixon. "Sandhill Potters Reviving Oldest of Arts in Jugtown," *News and Observer* (Raleigh), April 3, 1927.

Mercein, Eleanor. "Adventurous Cookery," *Ladies Home Journal* (March, 1933), pp. 12-13, 105-6, 109-10.

Mitchell, Joe Q. "Busbees Exhibit Art of Jugtown to Playmakers," *Chapel Hill Weekly*, February 17, 1928.

Noyce, Dorothy. "The Pottery of Jugtown," *Ford Times*, CI, No. 3 (March, 1959), 25-27.

"On and Off the Avenue," *The New Yorker*, II, No. 6 (March 27, 1926), 40.

Perry, Mavis. "Jugtown Ware," *News and Courier* (Charleston, S. C.), February 18, 1962.

Richards, M. C. "Leach: East and West," *Craft Horizons*, XX, No. 4 (July/August, 1960), 38.

Ries, Henrich. "Clay Deposits and Clay Industry in North Carolina," Bulletin 13, *North Carolina Geological Survey*, 1897.

Robertson, A. T., Jr. "Meet the Busbees, of Jugtown," *The State*, I, No. 25 (November 18, 1933), 16.

"Sandhill Potters Use Old Method, Turning Out Beautiful Pieces by Hand," *Philadelphia Inquirer*, April 24, 1938.

Sharpe, Bill. "Pottery-Making Preserved as an Art by the Busbees," *Greensboro Daily News*, April 24, 1938.

"Southerners Open Their Exposition: Industrial Story of 14 States is Told by Colorful Displays at Grand Central Palace," *New York Times*, May 12, 1925, p. 11.

Story, Hatcher P. "Lost N. C. Art is Made to Live Again; Pioneer Craft with A Pedigree: That Would Be Jugtown, U.S.A." *Charlotte Observer*, December 17, 1950.

Trenckmann, Clara. "Jugtown Potters Win Praise in Big N. Y. Exposition," syndicated article in *News and Observer* (Raleigh), May 31, 1925.

"Twin City Datebook," *Journal and Sentinel* (Winston-Salem), April 1, 1962.

Wolter, Beverly. "State's Pottery Art Faces a Crucial Era; Lack of Skilled Craftsmen Hits Home," *Journal and Sentinel* (Winston-Salem), September 1, 1963.

Wood, Ruth Kedzie. "Jugtown, Where They Make Jugs," *The Mentor*, XVI (April, 1928), 32-36.

Wright, Marion. "Arts and Artists," *Charlotte Observer*, January 7, 1940.

Legal Citations

Jugtown, Inc. v. *John Maré and The Jacques and Juliana Busbee's Jugtown, Inc.*, 6800, Office of the Clerk of Court, Moore County, North Carolina, Carthage.

Mrs. Louise R. Jordan, Next Friend of Juliana Busbee & Jugtown, Inc. v. John Maré & Jack & Juliana Busbee's Jugtown, Inc., 6826, Office of the Clerk of Court, Moore County, North Carolina, Carthage.

In the matter of Juliana Busbee, 7727, Office of the Clerk of Court, Moore County, North Carolina, Carthage.

"Articles of Incorporation of Jugtown, Incorporated," 86676, filed with the Secretary of State of North Carolina, March 12, 1959, Raleigh.

"Articles of Incorporation, Jacques & Juliana Busbee's Jugtown, Inc.," 86605, Book 6, p. 368, Office of the Clerk of Court, Moore County, North Carolina, March 11, 1959, Carthage.

Agreement of Lease, "W. H. Scott and Martha Jane Scott and Jacques Busbee," June 15, 1922 (in the files of John Maré).

Warranty Deed, "W. H. Scott and wife, Martha Jane Scott, to Jacques Busbee," Deed Book 94, p. 16, Office of the Register of Deeds, Moore County, North Carolina, August 25, 1924, Carthage.

Warranty Deed, "T. Franklin Scott and wife, Eula E. Scott, to Jacques Busbee," Deed Book 125, p. 416, Office of the Register of Deeds, Moore County, North Carolina, January 26, 1938, Carthage.

Warranty Deed, "Mrs. Juliana Busbee et al to Jugtown, Inc.," December 5, 1958, acknowledged before a Notary Public in Wake County, North Carolina, but unrecorded (in the files of Herbert F. Seawell, Jr.).

Warranty Deed, "Juliana Busbee to Jacques and Juliana Busbee's Jugtown, Inc.," Deed Book 228, p. 521, Office of the Register of Deeds, Moore County, North Carolina, March 11, 1959, Carthage.

Agreement between Juliana Busbee and John Maré, March 2, 1959 (in the files of P. H. Wilson, Carthage, N. C.). (Carbon copy.)

"Letters of Guardianship," Book 4, p. 48, Office of the Clerk of Court, Moore County, North Carolina, August 5, 1959, Carthage.

"Last Will and Testament of Jacques Busbee," 5757, Wills Book P, p. 92, Office of the Clerk of Court, Moore County, North Carolina, April 27, 1944, Carthage.

"Last Will and Testament of John Maré," 8369, Wills Book V, p. 511, Office of the Clerk of Court, Moore County, North Carolina, June 14, 1962, Carthage.

Unpublished Material

Busbee Letters, Woodrow W. Pruett Collection, Emporia, Virginia.

Busbee Papers, John Maré Collection, Southern Pines, North Carolina.

Busbee Papers, Blackwell P. Robinson Collection, Greensboro, North Carolina.

Jugtown Papers, Herbert F. Seawell, Jr., Files, Carthage, North Carolina.

Jugtown Papers, Jean Crawford Collection, Rowland, North Carolina.

Jugtown Papers, North Carolina Collection, University of North Carolina Library, Chapel Hill, North Carolina.

Jugtown Papers, North Carolina Department of Archives and History, Raleigh, North Carolina.

Jugtown Papers, North Carolina Museum of Art, Raleigh, North Carolina.

Jugtown Papers, P. H. Wilson Files, Carthage, North Carolina.

Pottery Industry Papers, North Carolina Collection, University of North Carolina Library, Chapel Hill, North Carolina.

Interviews

Braddy, Mamie H. Reporter for the *Journal and Sentinel* (Winston-Salem) and friend of the Busbees. Interview on June 22, 1962, Winston-Salem, N. C.

Bridges, William. Friend of Juliana Busbee. Interview on August 31, 1962, Lumberton, N. C.

Broughton, Howard C. Lawyer and executor of the estate of John Maré. Interviews on July 17, August 21, 1962, Southern Pines, N. C.

Burton, Ottway. Lawyer for Juliana Busbee for many years. Interview on August 21, 1962, Asheboro, N. C.

Manly, Frank. Preparator, North Carolina Museum of Art, and friend of Juliana Busbee, Interview on July 25, 1962, Raleigh, N. C.

Maré, John. Manager of Jugtown, 1959 to 1962. Interviews on October 27, November 3, 4, 1961; July 9, 1962, Southern Pines, N. C.

Owen, Ben. Master potter at Jugtown, 1923-1959. Now owner-manager of Ben Owen's Pottery. Interviews on October 7, 18, 27, November 3, 22, December 11, 1961; February 8, March 17, April 6, July 9, August 25, 1962, Seagrove, N. C.

Owen, Lucille. Wife of Ben Owen. Preserved papers on Jugtown and Ben Owen's pottery. Interviews on October 7, December 11, 1961, Seagrove, N. C.

Owen, Wade. Son of Ben Owen. Interview on August 21, 1962, Seagrove, N. C.

Owens, Bobby. Outside worker at Jugtown, beginning in 1960. Interview on August 25, 1962, Jugtown, N. C.

Owens, Vernon. Potter at Jugtown, beginning in 1960. Interview on August 25, 1962, Jugtown, N. C.

Pruett, Woodrow W. Friend of Juliana Busbee. Interview on August 31, 1962, Lumberton, N. C.

Resch, Mary John. Museum Assistant, Department of Archives and History, Raleigh. Interview on March 22, 1962.

Robinson, Blackwell P. Professor at The Woman's College of the University of North Carolina, Greensboro, and member of Jugtown, Incorporated. Interviews September, 1961-April, 1962.

Scott, Claud. Neighbor of the Busbees. Interview on October 27, 1961, Steeds, N. C.

Thompson, Clarence. Interior Designer. Friend of the Busbees since 1933. Owner of an outstanding collection of Jugtown Pottery, especially in blue-green. Interviews on July 17, 24, 1962, Southern Pines, N. C.

Thompson, Russell. Ceramist, a friend of the Busbees, and owner of a collection of Jugtown Pottery. Interviews on October 4, 1961; March 29, April 5, 1962, Greensboro, N. C.

Williams, Ben F. Curator, North Carolina Museum of Art, and a member of Jugtown, Incorporated. Interviews on October 2, December 13, 1961; January 25, March 22, July 19, 24, 1962, Raleigh, N. C.

Yow, Boyce. Fired kilns at Jugtown for several years. Interviews on October 18, November 22, 1961; February 8, 1962, Seagrove, N. C.